The Zero BS Guide on Creating Life Changing Income Using the Internet

The Simple Truth About Making Money On The Internet

How I Built an Online Empire

That Created Wealth, Freedom and

Prosperity in My Life

JUSTIN ANDREW SPENCER

By reading this e-book, you acknowledge that you have read, understood and agree to the following:

The Simple Truth About Making Money On The Internet is under the protection of copyright law. Any person who violates the law will be held accountable to the maximum fine and penalty issued by law.

This book was written with the intention to inform its readers of useful business principles and methodologies for making money online. The author and publisher make no claims that the reader will be able to use, understand or implement the ideas, methods or principles discussed or contained in whole or in part of this book.

The advice contained in this book should not be considered professional advice, but rather the opinions and experiences expressed solely by the author. The creator and producer of this publication make no guarantee you will achieve the same or similar results.

Although the techniques in this book were written to the best of the author's knowledge and ability, the author makes no guarantee that any piece of content in this book is accurate or complete. The level of results a person can achieve is relative and subject to their ability and intellect to apply the principles, methodologies and ideas described in this book.

The author and publisher make no guarantee or warranty for the information presented in this book and the author and publisher assume no liability for the application of any idea, method or principle in this book. Using the information in this book should be practiced at your sole digression and risk.

The author and the publisher will not be held liable or responsible for any loss or damages that appear to be tied or related to the information contained in this book. The reader

ISBN EBOOK: 978-0-9852462-0-4

ISBN PAPERBACK: 978-0-9852462-1-1

Stay *Connected* with Justin and *Learn* More:

www.ForeverProfitSystem.com

www.iJustinSpencer.com

www.Twitter.com/spencify

ACKNOWLEDGEMENTS

To *Dad*:

Thank you for teaching me important lessons about life and inspiring me to be great. You took control of your own life when you were very young. You did things unlike most people. You have always worked harder than anyone I know and there is a story well worth listening to behind everything you have done or created. You built your first empire when you were 19. It's only right that I strive to do the same.

To *Mom*:

Thank you for your prayers, your advice, your continued encouragement and your help. Not only have you have helped and raised me, but you have helped many other people as well, because you have a selfless nature about you. I look forward to making a positive impact on many people's lives, like you have done and continue to do every day. You have a big heart and I will do my best to help people and to help you.

To *Jules*:

You have been my best friend and partner for years. You have inspired me, motivated me and ushered me to keep going when I was out of breath. You are the smartest person I know and you are also fearless. You amaze me. You are going to be truly exceptional in everything you pursue in life. Thank you for being there for me and being an important part of my life and success in business.

To Ben:

Thank you for turbo charging my dreams and ambitions. You have been a great employer, business partner, mentor and friend. Only time will tell how far I can dig with the tools you have helped me sharpen.

To my parents,
Andrew Fatcheric and Jennifer Spencer

CONTENTS

"ATTENTION ALL AIRPORT PERSONNEL AND TRAVELERS, THE WEATHER CONDITIONS HAVE GONE FROM BAD TO WORSE. EXPECT FLIGHT DELAYS AND CANCELLATIONS."

One of my goals with this book was to make it fun to read. I did not have the desire to write a boring book with stale, regurgitated information because I felt that I would miss out on connecting with a lot of people. I'm not writing this book for the money—in all honesty I don't need it. I want to take you on an adventure.

My idea was to make this book a journey for you, to make it like a real experience as if it were something that actually happened to you. Instead of coming across a book claiming to have some sort of "ultimate formula", I want you to be part of the story and to experience the story with me. You will live with this experience and it will become a part of you and your life.

***

The steady clicking noise of the escalator moving upward seemed to churn into a rhythmic sort of tune. The smell of freshly brewed coffee invaded my nose and I could hear the sounds of shoes tapping against the floor around me and in the distance.

I looked up and saw the glass that displayed a pretty view of the darkened skyline. My feet were tired from standing and walking for most of the day and I felt exhausted. I considered sitting in a nearby massage chair but eventually I decided it was not necessary.

I just recently heard that the weather had taken a turn for the worse and I'm worried that my flight back home may have been delayed, or worse, canceled.

I made it to the top of the escalator and I noticed a circle of people staring at panels up on the wall that show the scheduled flight times and updates.

I walked over towards the group of people to see the status of my flight. I looked up and found out that my flight had been delayed 4 hours. My chest sunk and the carryon luggage I had been pulling seemed to feel even heavier.

A younger-looking guy who stood at about 5"11 with blond hair—wearing fitted designer clothes—was standing about 4 feet from the group and he looked over at me, and his quick eyes seemed to notice my fatigue and frustration.

He walked over to me and said reassuringly, "Don't worry, my flight got delayed a few hours too."

Trying to be polite, I joked back with him about having bad luck with traveling and the weather. He laughed and began tell me about a story where a 10 hour trip had turned into an 18 hour twisted passage.

After a few minutes, he offered to buy me a coffee and I took him up on his offer because I was very tired and wouldn't mind having some caffeine to keep me awake.

He invited me to sit down with him and he began making conversation by asking me what I did for a living and where I was headed before the flight became delayed.

I told him I was headed back home and I was in between jobs, searching for a more permanent employment position; I told him I was trying to find a job that paid more because I wanted to have more freedom, I wanted more options.

I went on making small talk when I suddenly started realizing more things about this person.

The caffeine from the coffee he bought me had made me alert once again. This guy looked like he was maybe 19, or 20 years old, tops. Whenever he answered a question or asked a question he sounded so matter-of-fact or sure of himself.

And when I first saw him I had noticed he was wearing clothes that probably cost more than my car. Who was I talking to? I suddenly realized that I wanted to know what this guy did for a living. How is a kid this young, traveling and offering drinks and purchasing designer clothes? My curiosity started to become overwhelming.

I had never seen him before, so I ruled out the fact that he might be in the entertainment industry. A few seconds had gone by as I was processing this and he seemed to notice I was having an internal discussion with myself.

His eyebrows creased and then he smirked because he must have known what I was curious about.

“What’s on your mind?” he said casually, pretending as if he didn’t already know.

I clarified our mental conversation out loud.

“I was just curious, about what it is you do?” I said trying to sound casual.

“It’s hard to describe what I do because you have to have a background in my type of business to adequately understand what it is I do” Justin said.

“I think I can keep up” I said with confidence.

He took a sip of his $10 latte and said “Alright then, let’s start from the beginning.”

***

"A man who does not follow his wildest dreams is left with wonder for what he could have become."

~Justin A. Spencer

A Walk That Changed My Life

Let me paint the scene for you. It was December 9th, 2010. Class was in session.

I picked up my pen as the exam slid onto my desk. A flutter of anxiety, a nervous tick, passed through my shoulders and down to my feet, much like the type of shiver you get on occasion that causes your body to shake rapidly for a second.

The time was 9 o'clock a.m. I had been awake for 26 hours without sleep, 10 of those hours spent studying for this exam because it would determine my grade in C++ Objective Programming II.

Minutes turned into seconds.

My mind had become foggy and my focus distorted, as the professor warned us we had 10 minutes left. The clock was ticking but my brain was not. The pressure was taking advantage of me and I struggled to focus.

My anxiety started to show colors of frustration and anger.

I felt the sting of shame penetrate my confidence. I had only filled out half of the exam. This was more than a test. This test would affect my entire grade point average and my grade point average would determine my ability to attain a scholarship and financial aid.

A lot was riding on these last few moments.

During these last 10 minutes I gave the exam my absolute best effort. I brought the exam to the desk of my professor and he proceeded to grade it. The clock suddenly started ticking slower.

Eons pass. Then at long last, he hands the exam back to me. Facedown, so my colleagues cannot see my performance.

I took a small step back, and flipped the exam.

My stomach seemed to cringe at the circled red number looking back at me. My throat clamped up as if I were about to give a public speech.

"Justin, I think it best if you stop by my office at some point, soon."

After clearing my throat, I managed to say, "Yeah sure, I'll stop by."

The cold sting of wintertime New York awakened me out of my trance. I walked quickly across the snow-covered campus until I made it to my car. I opened the door and jumped inside quickly to escape the wind.

I rubbed my hands together for a brief moment to create some heat, then picked up my keys and fumbled through them until I found my car key.

I inserted the key into the ignition and twisted it gently, expecting to hear the rumble of the engine cylinders fire up. Nothing happened. I dismissed the first try as a fluke and tried to start the engine once again. Nothing.

The flush of nervousness and frustration came back to accompany me all too soon. I was scheduled to work at both of my jobs today. I was running on zero sleep and now my car would not start.

My first instinct was to go back inside the nearest building because it was freezing outside. I did not know if a dead battery was the issue, but in the past I had replaced the alternator that charges the battery, so I knew that could potentially be the problem if the used replacement had stopped working. A jump may have only gotten me a few miles if that was the issue.

I dosed off in a chair in one of the student lobbies. Two hours passed and I was finally able to get a ride home from my friend. He left me at home and went to work.

Best Buy will want to know why I am running late, so I call my manager and explain the situation; he knows I am on my way. My roommate is at work, my work clothes are on and I now I begin the 3 mile jog to the plaza behind the mall.

25 minutes pass. I made it. I'm cold but sweating, an awful feeling. The environment of the store was not sympathetic. All hell slowly broke loose.

Angry customers harass me about refunds and claims of defective appliances. I search through their words carefully. I find contradictions in their claims. I explain to them the store policy and why they are not permitted to obtain a refund for their circumstance. I politely apologize. This doesn't work.

The manager now listens to one customer's story. He reiterates the store policy that the customer knows well by now. Finally, the customer leaves. My manager and I make a few snide jokes to diffuse the situation.

It is now 4:00. I have to be at Cracker Barrel by 5:00. I check the schedule and no one else is off the clock. Everyone else is scheduled to work until close.

I have to walk, again.

I threw on my coat and gazed outside. The weather was not on my side. Cracker Barrel was slightly under a mile away, but I could tell I was in for a nasty trip.

The sun had left the sky and the day had turned darker, colder, and lonelier. The wind was madness. It stung my eyes, it burned my face and it threatened to blow me over. It felt like I was in the middle of a snow storm in Alaska. I inhaled a deep breath of crisp frozen air and bent my legs to regain stability. I walked with my head down trying to shelter my face and ears from the gusts of razor-sharp cold air.

I made it to the bridge that passes over an interstate highway leading to my destination. The wind blows the snow off the top of a nearby snow bank into my face and it becomes hard to see. I blink repeatedly to recover my vision. The only thing I could see was my breath in front of my face.

The temperature was below freezing and the wind chill factor made the air temperature feel like it was in the negatives. I had left Best Buy only a few minutes ago and it felt like I had been walking for an eternity.

I was halfway across the bridge that lead to the restaurant when a sudden heavy stream of wind caused me to start jogging to get to Cracker Barrel sooner.

My shoe must have caught a patch of ice because the next thing I knew was that I was doing the chicken dance to stay up without falling. I fell forward and caught myself with my hands. Stupidly, I was not wearing gloves. My hands turned to ice. My lungs started to feel heavy, my feet felt like stones. My shoes were drenched with wet snow and my face was numb and throbbing.

I could barely pick myself up. I was exhausted. I had 1 hour of sleep in a chair between yesterday morning and today. As if I could handle the firepower of the wind already, the mother of all wind gusts threatened to put my face right back on the ice covered cement.

I was a guy—a confident guy, filled with pride. I did not cry much. But, if there was ever a time for feeling weak, this surely was it. I started to tear up, but not because of the wind. I could not help feeling sorry for myself. I don't ever purposefully try to take pity on myself, but for this moment I felt defeated.

I stopped walking. I stood there, in the middle of the cold winter night. The self pity that had been sweeping over me because I was weak started to take a new form. As the winter storm outside raged on, a storm was beginning to take form inside of me.

I looked up towards the sky and yelled as loud as I could,

"WHY AM I ******* WALKING IN A ******* BLIZZARD?"

A spiral of anger had been pushed down full throttle.

If the windows of the few cars daring to drive in this weather were not sealed shut, the drivers passing by would have surely heard me.

I guess when you arrive at your lowest point in life, you can only go up.

This is when it happened. This is when I felt it. Instinct or intuition or subconscious, I don't know what it was, but I sensed it and I felt different. Standing in the lonely winter darkness, I realized I was responsible.

I was responsible for the defective car I drove. I was responsible for selecting which career to pursue. I chose to work two jobs and go to college. I chose to move here. I did what everyone told me I should do. I did what I was expected to do. I went to college, took out 6 separate loans to cover the tuition and this was only year 2. As I realized this, the rage surging through the blood my heart was pumping so violently finally began to cool down. I had realized something truly fascinating.

The obvious solution was standing in front of me, before my very eyes. It was so simple, yet so beautiful and obvious that is was hidden in plain sight. My turning point realization was this: I had a choice.

I repeated this out loud a few times as if someone had told me about this great hidden secret for the first time.

I then understood there was a difference between doing what you desire and what you are expected to do. I never desired these choices I had made. Perhaps I thought I did, but it was evident now that I did not do what I should have done. An unfamiliar warmth circulated throughout my body to my outer limbs.

I looked out into the distance from the bridge and shining through the darkness of the winter cold was a glowing red sign. By squinting and wiping the water seeping from my eyes I could just barely make out that it was a hotel. A luxurious one at that. I had recalled seeing it before; it was the type of place you stayed at if you were rich.

I managed to crack a private joke: "I wonder how many ***** you have to **** to stay at a place like that?" Although it should have been impossible, I managed to smile.

"I could choose to be rich." I said out loud.

The hotel sign glowing back at me in the distance looked like a sign of hope, a symbol, a goal, a turning point, a new chapter for a new beginning. The smile that crossed my face had become strengthened. Behind that smile was a determination that had been created by a series of events.

I could not get rid of that smile if I had tried.

I was invincible.

The lonely road of the winter darkness was becoming full of **light**.

The residue of the events that had taken a toll on me had formed a new me.

I don't remember much that occurred at Cracker Barrel that night. I don't recall if the customers were rude. I don't remember if I received good tips and I don't remember what time I finally made it there.

What I do remember was the cold winter walk that changed my life, and the feeling I had when I was walking there: a feeling of hope, possibility and freedom.

***

Justin stopped talking and slid out of the booth.

"Wait Justin, what ended up happening?" I asked quickly.

"Oh, hold on I'll get to that, I have to use the men's room." He smirked and walked away. After a few minutes he came back and slid back into the booth.

"So what ended up happening after that night at Cracker Barrel?" I asked again, my excitement was shining through my words.

"Basically, I ended up dropping out of college and I quit both of my jobs because I learned how to create businesses that get customers by means of the internet" he said once again sounding all-to-casual.

"How often do you work? Or do you have to…work?" I asked, trying to hide my excitement.

"No, not really, I choose to work when I feel like it. I actually like working, to be honest, but I like traveling more. I can actually work while I travel if I want to", he said correcting himself.

"If you don't mind me asking, how much can you make building these businesses?" I asked hoping he didn't think I was prying.

"Whatever you want. The sky is the limit really. I make well into the 5 figure mark each month but I have met people who make 7 and even 8 figures a month". He said once again, all-to-casually.

I started thinking to myself how amazing it must feel to be in his shoes. I was debating whether or not to be envious, annoyed, or happy to be in his presence. I can't get over the fact that he is casually disclosing that he makes more in one month then some people do in…wow.

I kept speculating to myself and I decided to remain skeptical. He automatically noticed my internal conflict, again.

I looked up at him and he smiled as if he had recognized my confused expression from somewhere else, like he had seen it before.

"I can explain to you what it is I do and how I do it. It is actually, embarrassingly simple."

He took another sip of his latte and said "Well, are you up for it?"

I acted like I was trying to make up my mind and finally I admitted that I was curious and I wanted to understand this mystery.

"I'm ready – let's go" I said edging him on to explain to me the unknown.

And so our journey begins…

***

"Learning new information is the enemy of negative thoughts, barriers and problems. You learn by reading and asking yourself questions."

~Justin A. Spencer

The Question: What Do I Do and How Do I Do It?

The answer to this question is much simpler than one might think. It really is, quite honestly, embarrassingly simple.

These are the 4 most basic ways you can make money on the internet *without* working for someone else. For example, this list does not include work-from-home jobs where you are employed by a company or working as a freelancer.

First – What is internet marketing? If you are doing internet marketing you are selling something using the internet to advertise what it is you are selling.

Here are the 4 ways internet marketers "make money online".

1) *Selling Advertising Space* – You can build websites and sell a square of space on your site to other businesses who want to advertise their products and services. You have options based on how you would prefer to be paid. You can earn money each time an Ad is clicked on or you can charge a monthly, weekly or daily fee for keeping the Ad on your website.

2) *Affiliate Marketing* – You can play the role of a virtual salesman that gets paid a commission for selling a product or service for a business. You can refer customers to any company that has an online affiliate program. You can also refer customers to other brick and mortar businesses that have websites where internet traffic can interact with the website in order to sign up for a service or make a product purchase.

3) *Information Marketing* – The third way to make money using the internet is by selling information to people (that you have produced and own) in the form of physical materials, or digital materials, plain and simple. This includes books, courses, e-books, audio discs, videos, DVD's, etc.

4) *E-Commerce* – This method involves taking your entire store or business online. Amazon is a perfect example. You employ the internet as your primary advertising channel and you can sell pretty much anything.

Let's take a further look into the simple truth about making money on the internet.

The internet is the world we live in, connected. What this means is that business owners now have the ability to expand their reach to get customers beyond the physical barriers of location. "Making money online" or "making money on the internet" means that you are doing one of the 4 models described above.

If you own a brick and mortar business and you have a website, then this means you are using the internet as one of your advertising options to reach your customers.

An "offline" type of business is a business that focuses primarily on reaching customers without establishing a huge presence on the internet as a primary tool for doing so. Brick and mortar businesses that are dependent on physical interaction with the customer will limit the amount of customers the internet can bring to that particular business.

Thus, advertising in local media channels is a more sensible approach for some small business owners and an "online" or "internet" based business uses the internet as its primary advertising/marketing channel to reach customers.

There are more ways to advertise a business to attract customers than by simply using the internet. Any business can engage in many other channels of advertising such as: radio, TV, newspaper, direct mail, yellow pages, billboards, sponsorships and the list goes on.

The correct way to describe making money on the internet goes like this:

"I make money online by building website based businesses that sell stuff to customers browsing throughout the internet."

Second – What is marketing in general? Marketing is the art of selling. Marketing is the art of getting customers to sign up for your services or persuading them to buy your products. With the internet, you can build websites that perform the art of selling. Websites do not get tired and go to sleep. They do not get hungry or take a shower. They do not need to exercise or take breaks. They can perform the art of selling 24/7/365. This is why you hear about all of these "Get Rich Schemes" explaining to you how you can make money while you are on vacation, or sleeping, or walking your dog.

As long as you have traffic coming to your websites, you will have customers paying you for answering their problems with a solution, while performing the art of selling effectively.

Since you are selling something, you are doing business. Therefore, you own multiple businesses because you are either selling ad space or selling your own products or services or selling someone else's products or services, period.

How Do I Do It?

How I do it is the premise of this entire book. There are some things you will need to know before I can explain to you the best way to create an income that will change your life. Let's embark on our journey now and I will explain to you how I use the models described and you will see why my methods work—very well.

Part 1: An Introduction to Search Advertising

Chapter 1: Search Concepts

"A search engine is like a librarian and the World Wide Web is like a library."
~Justin A. Spencer

Understanding Search

A search engine is basically an archaeologist or a librarian. It searches through every single page that exists on the internet and then remembers all of the pages that it finds.

It will then categorize each page, so that when someone is looking for information that may be on a particular page, the engine with then provide you with the link or address of that page so that you can access it and learn more about what you were searching for.

It is a beautiful invention, and naturally an amazing avenue to control the internet. Google is the most highly used website/service on the internet and if I am not mistaken, in the world.

Google was not the first search engine ever created, however they have done a better job at providing a superior search service, so they rose to the throne as the most used search service available.

The opportunities that search engines like Google have created for businesses are like a dream. It does not matter whether you are attracting customers with paid advertising (PPC) or a free organic listing (SEO). Search engine platforms act as gateways to your business, in that they are the key to a limitless number of potential customers. Whether you get ranked for a high volume keyword organically (SEO) or whether you write a winning text ad, (PPC) your ability to attract a continuous stream of customers is huge.

Search traffic is one of the best sources of traffic because people are already interested in whatever it is you have to sell. Look at it from the flip perspective: imagine trying to sell something to somebody who is not interested in what you are selling. Sometimes we can be persuaded to get interested; however that is a whole additional process.

Having "warm" or genuinely interested customers lining up to take a look at what you have to offer them is an amazing thing and it provides us the ability to create profitable businesses out of thin air. Interested traffic = quality traffic.

Different phases (levels) of interest

- Phase 1: Web searcher has a genuine interest; they are seeking more information on a product or service but are not ready to make a buying decision.
- Phase 2: Web searcher already has the information and he/she is now trying to decide which place or which company they should choose to buy from. This is a product review type phase.
- Phase 3: This phase is so close to phase 2 that it might as well be tied together with it. The searcher has uncovered a product review and now is planning to go to the source to make a purchase of that product or service.
- Phase 4: The searcher becomes a buyer.

Types of Search Based Business Models

SEO (Search Engine Optimization) Model

A SEO business model involves getting ranked for keywords organically. This means that you do not have to pay for your traffic; this is a free listing sponsored by Google because Google's search engine algorithm found your website to be relevant enough to the search term query to be displayed on the front page listings.

This is applicable to Yahoo and Bing, although getting ranked on the first page of Google is much more important than getting ranked on the front page of Yahoo or Bing. This is simply because Google receives a lot more traffic than Yahoo and Bing.

If you get ranked on the first page of Google then it is likely that you will be ranked on the first page of Yahoo and Bing as well. But it is also important to understand that Google, Yahoo and Bing do not have the same search algorithms. This means that how Google decides to rank your site is different than how Bing or Yahoo would decide to rank your site.

The algorithms of each search engine have different priorities has far as how relevant a website is in relation to the keyword, among many other variables. This is why you can be ranked higher or lower on a different search engine. For example, your website could be ranked in the 24th position on Google and the 16th Position on Bing and the 32nd position on Yahoo for the same search query.

The search algorithms do have commonalities, but it is important to understand that they are not the exactly the same. Based on my experiences with SEO, I have a theory that Bing and Yahoo take into account the name of your domain (website address) in relation to the relevancy of the keyword you are competing for more so than Google does.

Here is what I mean by that:

If your domain name is HowToRideYourBike.com and a Bing searcher searches the keyword: "How to ride your bike" then your website would be more likely to have a better position on Bing or Yahoo than on Google.

Exact match domains are important when considering the SEO business model. We will go into much greater detail on this in (Part 2: The Process of Search Engine Optimization).

The obvious advantage of an SEO based model is that you do not have to pay for your traffic, so there is much less risk that you will lose money upfront.

Pay Per Click (PPC) Model

The pay per click search model involves writing ads and selecting corresponding keywords to trigger your ads that you bid on. Advertising platforms such as Google Adwords and Microsoft Adcenter are by far the most popular.

When you use Google, Yahoo or Bing to search for information, 90% of the time you will see “sponsored results” listings in the top most part and the right side of the results listings page.

Here is an example screenshot:

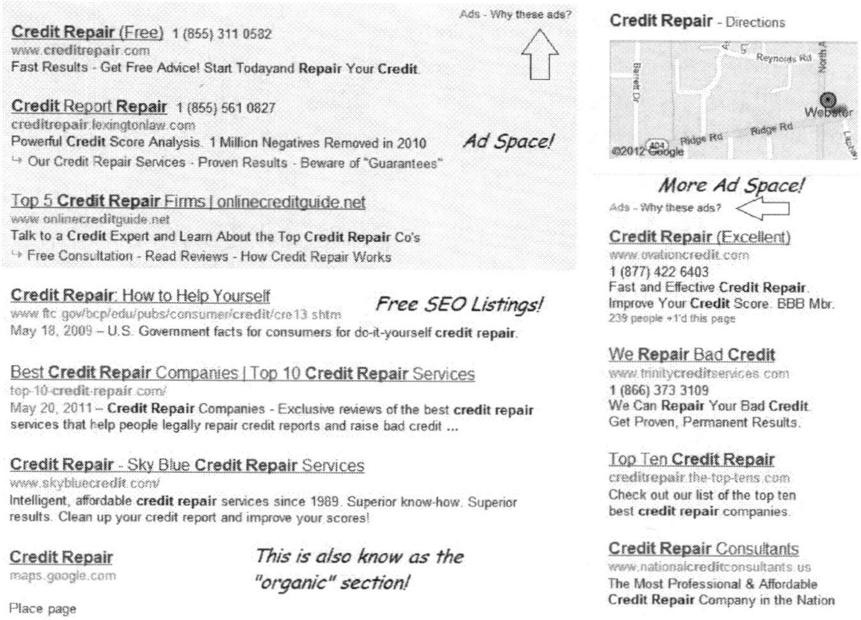

This example shows the current results for the keyword “credit repair”. These listings are ads from advertisers using Google Adwords. Likewise, Microsoft Adcenter is the platform for serving your ads on Yahoo and Bing.

This search business model is a bit more mathematical because you have to calculate your advertising costs and sales revenue in order to determine if your ad listing is creating a profit margin. Or in other words, your profits or take home pay is the result of what is left over after you subtract your ad spending from your sales revenue.

For example: Let's say that you are selling toothbrushes. Every time you sell one toothbrush you earn approximately $10.00. If you spend $30 to make 4 sales then you have earned a profit of $10.00 and your ad listing is creating an actual profit for you.

If you spend $30 to make $40, how many times would you spend $30 to make $40 if you had a choice? Well, you do have a choice, and if you scale that exact campaign, which means to essentially create more volume, then you can spend $300 per day to make $400 per day. This is $3,000.00 per month and $36,000.00 per year in profit, just from selling a toothbrush.

Although doing this sounds easy in theory, it is much harder to get a campaign running that stays consistent like this every day for a year. However this does not mean that it is impossible. In order to build a campaign like this, we need to have the proper tool set and we have to understand a few key concepts to make dozens of campaigns like this.

The obvious advantage about this model is that it takes much less time to actually receive traffic than an SEO driven model. The side effect is that you can lose money upfront, before your campaign becomes profitable. We will venture much deeper into how to set up profitable campaigns and to scale them in (Part 3: On Pay Per Click Advertising).

***

Connecting the dots

- *Search traffic is high quality because the searchers are already interested in what you have to offer them.*
- *Search Engine Optimization (SEO) is one method of getting traffic from search engines like Google, Yahoo and Bing. You do not have to pay for this method of advertising.*
- *Pay Per Click (PPC) involves placing bids on keywords and writing ads to be triggered based on the keyword. You pay each time your ad is clicked.*

Part 2: The Process of Search Engine Optimization (SEO)

Chapter 2: The Importance of Traffic and Research

"Diligence is the mother of good luck."
~Benjamin Franklin

Importance of traffic

Many SEO-based marketing businesses have been created around one keyword. Focusing on a single search phrase will allow your job to become much easier. Remember, to own a successful business, the only requirement is that you are selling something and turning a profit from whatever it is you are selling. It doesn't matter if you are selling someone else's product or service or your own product or service.

There are an incredible amount of individuals out there who have literally made millions off of product referrals, service referrals and advertising revenues all from super simple, basic little websites that have a consistent flow of traffic.

There is an important concept to understand here, and it is this: you can pay a graphic designer $12,000 to create the best possible looking website on planet Earth, but if that website is not receiving any traffic at all, then that $12,000 website is good for nothing.

However if you have a $15 website that gets 3,000 hits a month, then you have a profitable marketing business in your arsenal. With that being said, your website graphics are not as important as how popular the site itself is in terms of traffic.

You cannot have a brick and mortar business without repeat/loyal customers. Likewise you cannot have a successful website marketing business without continuous traffic flow. I have seen basic, even ugly websites generate so much money that I would have never thought possible simply because web searchers were able to find the ugly website on Google. So the key point here is that getting traffic is 100 times more important than having a pretty website.

But don't get the wrong idea. You can have 12,000 hits a month to your website but if your website is bad at performing the art of selling to that traffic (prospects) then you have a problem—however that sort of problem is 100 times easier to fix.

Importance of research

Now that we know traffic is the most important ingredient for a profitable marketing business, the question becomes: How do we make sure our websites get traffic? Let me tell you something—if you understand how to get traffic to your site, that is 95% of the battle to creating any profitable business.

In order to create a website that gets traffic, you have to do your homework. You have to get down and dirty and do a little bit of research so you know which search terms (keywords) to target in order to get traffic to your site from the search engines like Google, Yahoo, Bing, AltaVista, Dogpile, Ask, AOL, and AVG. The most important engine is Google, but my point is that there are many search engines.

In order to do this efficiently you will need a keyword research tool. There are many available out there, but I choose to use the Google keyword tool. The Google keyword tool is not 100% accurate, but then again no keyword search tool is.

The Google keyword tool will give you a list of 800 ideas/suggestions based on the seed keyword you are researching. So if you type the keyword "weight loss" into the Google keyword research tool, the software will return the metrics of that keyword and approximately 800 variations and metrics for closely related keywords. This tool helps make informed decisions about which keywords to use when building your websites.

Doing research for the proper keywords is a crucial step in the process of building a successful marketing business. We will explore the characteristics of keywords that make them easy to get ranked and therefore allow us to get traffic to make money on our websites. We will refer to keywords that have these characteristics as "profitable keywords". See the screenshot below to see what the keyword tool looks like:

The keyword tool will give you up to 800 keyword ideas (depending on how broad the seed keyword is). You can see how competitive it is to get traffic from web searchers searching keywords containing the phrase "weight loss".

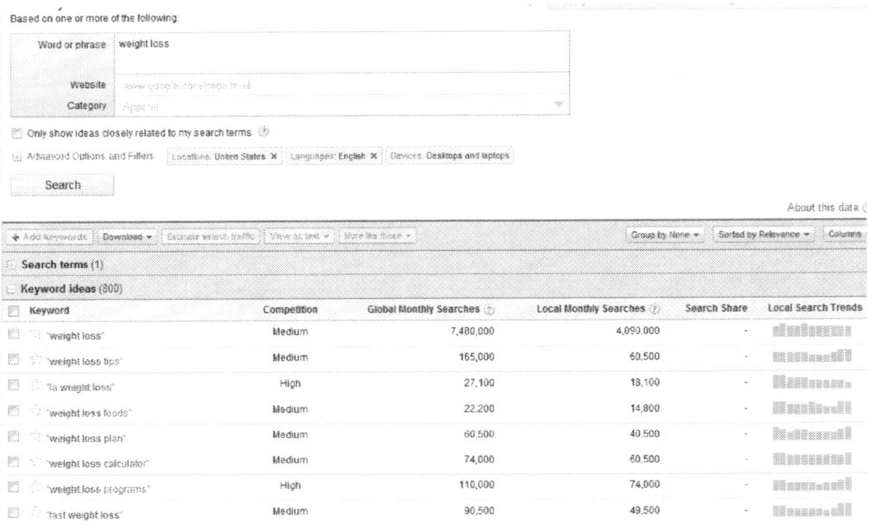

Looking at the results chart from left to right: the *keyword* is the phrase or sentence that is searched in Google. The *competition* is an indicator of how many web pages on the internet are competing to get ranked for the keyword. The *global monthly searches* are the monthly search volume for the keyword on an international level. The *local monthly searches* are for the U.S. only. *Local search trends* are how consistent the volume remains on a month to month basis for the U.S.

Characteristics of a profitable keyword

When I do keyword research, I dig as deep as possible into my niche (category) to see if I can uncover little gems that I can use to get traffic to my new sites. This is the most important part of an SEO model—get this wrong and you could experience utter disappointment and more importantly – zero cash inflow.

Here are the four main characteristics of a profitable keyword

1. Keyword competition: This metric is determined by how many other pages on the World Wide Web are competing for slots or positions for that keyword. The best way to ensure that the keyword you are doing research on is profitable for you is to make sure that it has less than 100,000 competing web pages. One method of doing this is to go to a search engine (preferably Google) and type your keyword in quotes (as pictured below) and press enter to do a search. If the number of competing pages that show up is less than 100k, then the keyword passes stage 1 of the profitability test.

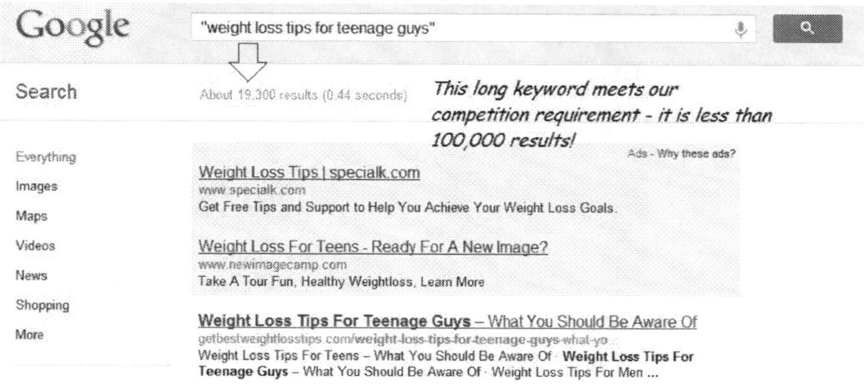

2. Keyword search volume: If your keyword has low competition but no volume at all, then it does not pass this stage of phase of the profitable keyword test. Getting ranked for terms that no one ever searches is relatively pointless. Some SEO professionals argue that Google appreciates the fact that you are ranked first for something, whether it is searched for or not. However I personally don't think this will make or break your site and

I do not believe it is worth the money, time or effort to invest in a keyword is never searched for. It won't make you money.

This keyword (Weight Loss Tips for Teenage Guys) has less than 300 hits per month, which means I would not build an entire website around it. Instead, I would make a single page on a website targeted towards this keyword—not the whole website itself.

Let me clarify the difference: look back at the screenshot displaying the competition requirement. The website ranked #1 for this keyword phrase is: GetBestWeightLossTips.com/*Weight-Loss-Tips-For-Teenage-Guys...*

The person who owns this site created a page with the purpose to get that page ranked for this one keyword. Basing an entire site around one seed keyword would mean you want to register a domain name with the seed keyword in it, for example, WeightLossTipsForTeenageGuys.com (more on this soon).

3. <u>Search Patterns (Trends):</u> When researching, you will notice some keywords have more of a fad type of search pattern. By taking a quick look at the trend readings you should be able to determine if the keyword is consistently searched on a month to month basis or not. It makes little sense to build your business around a keyword that may not be "in style" every month. A keyword that gets 50,000 searches in one month and 200 searches the next is way too inconsistent.

Keyword	Competition	Global Monthly Searches	Local Monthly Searches	Search Share	Local Search Trends
"snookie weight loss"	Low	2,400	1,900	-	
"snookie lost weight"	Low	590	390	-	

Way too inconsistent! We want longetivity!

4. Nature of the Keyword: If the keyword we are researching has no competition and a decent search volume then this brings us to the nature of the keyword itself. So if we figure out that the keyword "milk" has 87,000 competing pages and 2,600 searches a month, we have to analyze the nature of the keyword itself. In all honesty this 4th phase is put into place to see how much revenue you can expect from this type of keyword. I honestly am not quite sure how I would make money by being ranked for the keyword "milk". What I mean is the keyword "milk" is not a buyer keyword. The keyword doesn't involve interest in anything; it's just a silly keyword that is very broad and vague.

Now this doesn't mean you can't be creative with these types of keywords, especially since other marketers tend to ignore them. If you had "milk" keyword traffic, you could make your site into some form of quiz page, like "How much do you know about milk?" and gather visitor data to send to other companies related or not related to milk at all. If someone Googles the keyword "milk", that person is probably just bored—however, that person has other interests or things that he/she likes.

So the purpose of a site ranked for the keyword "milk" could be for entertainment. It all depends on how you look at it. If you can slant something that is normally not interesting into something interesting then you can surely turn a profit from it. This takes a little bit of creativity, but if you develop a creative edge doing stuff like in this example, that will serve you as an incredible asset.

On the opposite end of the spectrum, if you find a keyword that has 14,000 competing pages, 6,000 monthly searches and the nature of the keyword implies that it is a buyer keyword, then you have stumbled upon a little treasure that can make you a very large amount of money.

For example, let us suppose that the keyword "buy charcoal netbook cover" had those characteristics. This surely could become a huge SEO cash asset. The only things left to do are to set up the website and connect your affiliate links to the charcoal netbook cover product (or by using a different method of income creation). Amazon has tons of products like this and they have an affiliate program. I actually just bought a leather charcoal travel case for my new Kindle Fire at Amazon the other day!

Also, just because the keyword phrase had the word “buy” in it does not mean that this is a requirement to be a “buyer keyword”. But that certainly helps, because it clearly spells out the fact that the person wants to buy something.

Keyword match types

Search terms (3)

Keyword	Competition	Global Monthly Searches	Local Monthly Searches	Search Share	Local Search Trends
weight loss	Medium	11,100,000	7,480,000	-	
[weight loss]	High	201,000	90,500	-	
"weight loss"	Medium	7,480,000	4,090,000	-	

Go to page: 1 Show rows: 100 1 - 3 of 3

In the above screenshot you can see the keywords:

- weight loss
- [weight loss]
- “weight loss”

Let’s explore the differences between these three examples.

First: Broad Match

First on the list is what is called a broad match keyword. A broad match keyword is not depicted by brackets or quotes and indicates how many searches on a monthly basis the contents of the seed keyword are searched. This is why broad match will always have the highest volume count out of the 3 match types.

Let’s look at some examples of broad match keywords for our seed keyword, which is *weight loss*:

- Fast **weight loss** dieting pills
- Best **weight** dieting **loss** solution
- Strawberry **loss** mango **weight** drink

As you can see, any keyword search query that contains the contents of the seed keyword will be added into the monthly volume hit counter. The contents of the seed keyword do not need to be in order, and they do not have to be relevant to anything else inside the search query sentence. So for the purpose of doing keyword research, broad match is a bad indicator of search volume.

Just look at this. According to Google, the following keyword has 40,500/searches per month for the broad match:

Keyword	Competition	Global Monthly Searches	Local Monthly Searches	Search Share	Local Search Trends
way to save money	Medium	40,500	33,100	-	
[way to save money]	Medium	260	140	-	
"way to save money"	Medium	8,100	5,400	-	
ways to save money	Medium	165,000	110,000	-	
[ways to save money]	Medium	14,800	9,900	-	
"ways to save money"	Medium	40,500	27,100	-	

The broad match keyword *Way to save money* makes up 40,500 searches out of 165,000 searches for the broad match keyword: *Ways to save money.* The only difference between the keyword searches is the plural "s" on *ways.*

My point with the example in the above screenshot is that the [exact] and "phrase" matches of the same keyword are much lower. Basing your site around a keyword from broad match statistics is a bad idea, always.

It is important to wrap your mind around how Google takes into account the volume counters for keywords so you don't misinterpret a bad keyword for a good one (in terms of volume).

Second: [Exact] Match

For [Exact] matches, nothing but the seed keyword *weight loss* matters—this indicates the metrics for the exact search query with no variations. So if someone Googles the term *weight loss*, and that's it, then that is an exact match.

Only looking at data (searches per month/competition) for the [exact] match gives you far too conservative of a number and does not show the full potential of the keyword, nor does it give you accurate competition results.

Third: "Phrase" Match

The "phrase" match, listed in quotation marks, is like broad match, except the seed keyword has to be in the proper order, which means *weight* comes first and *loss* comes second, and there are no words in between them.

Let's look at some examples:

- The best **weight loss** program
- Total fitness plan for gym or at home **weight loss**
- **Weight loss** dieting pills for belly fat removal

Further clarification: Why you need to do research in "phrase" match only

You want to know how many websites you are competing with that contain the keyword phrase that you are interested in ranking for. It is highly likely you will get traffic to your website based on variations of your chosen keyword. Phrase matches allow room for search variations while being more relevant than broad match searches.

For example, let's say we own the domain WeightLoss.com.

If the primary keyword we can get traffic for is *weight loss* then the phrase match is the best indicator of how much traffic we can receive—not exact and not broad match types. This is because we can get traffic for any of the following phrase based keywords:

- The best **weight loss** pills
- Top 10 list of **weight loss** diets
- **Weight loss** exercise programs

We are not limited to just [weight loss] (the one keyword), and broad match contains less relevant searches. Since broad match is literally too broad, and exact is too granular (specific), the phrase match of the keyword we want to get ranked for is the designated middleman.

This is why we do a "phrase" match competition peak in Google to see what the results returned for the keyword are, and not an [exact] match or broad match:

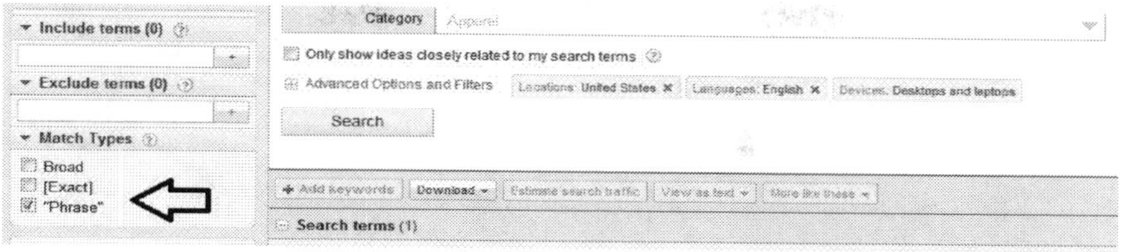

***

Connecting the dots

- *An ugly site with traffic can be profitable. A beautifully designed website without traffic is useless.*
- *Doing proper keyword research is absolutely vital to your success.*
- *Make sure that whenever you build a keyword-based SEO website that it meets the three main criteria for getting traffic:*
  1) Under 100,000 competing pages for the: "keyword"
  2) 300+ searches per month for the: "keyword"
  3) Consistent search trend

Chapter 3: It's Not How You Use It, But How You Name It

"Domain name relevance is a priceless asset when doing the process of SEO."
~Justin A. Spencer

The domain name is very important in the SEO model. The domain name should be relevant to whatever the site is about.

In my personal opinion, I feel that just being "relevant" or "related" is not enough. So if possible, when I find a keyword that has criteria that I consider to be profitable, I like to name the domain right after it.

So your ideal domain looks like this: www.YourKeyword.com

When we spoke about the "buy charcoal netbook cover" example, the ideal domain name to get traffic from that keyword would simply be: BuyCharcoalNetbookCover.com

Now I do have restrictions on this. I normally only ever rent domain names with the following extensions: (ordered by the most preferred at the top)

1. .com (commercial)
2. .net (network)
3. .org (organization)
4. .info (information)

I have gotten a .biz (business) domain name extension ranked on the first page of Google before, but I am still skeptical of whether or not Google's search algorithm is biased towards certain domain name extensions.

The domain name was StabilityRunningShoes.biz and the keyword was "Stability Running Shoes". The competition was 187,000 competing pages, which is too high, but the volume looked good at around 6,600 searches per month.

I wish I had known back then to check the number of competing web pages for that particular phrase. I am ranked #8 which is the last listing on the first page for the keyword. There are a ton of ingredients that the search engines look at when ranking websites and extension is most likely not as significant as I speculate. But nevertheless, I usually stick to buying a domain with one of the four extensions listed above.

***

Connecting the dots

- *Your domain name should be YourKeyword.com or a close variation.*
- *Stick with the four common extensions: .com, .net, .org, and .info*
- *By not properly assessing my competition with my running shoe site, it took much longer to get it ranked on the first page and it cost a lot of money*

Chapter 4: What is My Report Card?

The importance of page rank

A page rank is a numerical grade, much like a report card, that search engines like Google assign to your website. Google's page rank algorithm looks at quite a few pieces of information to form a numerical grade for your website. The grading system ranges from 0 – 10. Zero being the lowest and ten meaning the website's contribution to the world is way beyond average.

You can check the page rank grade of your website at: www.prchecker.net

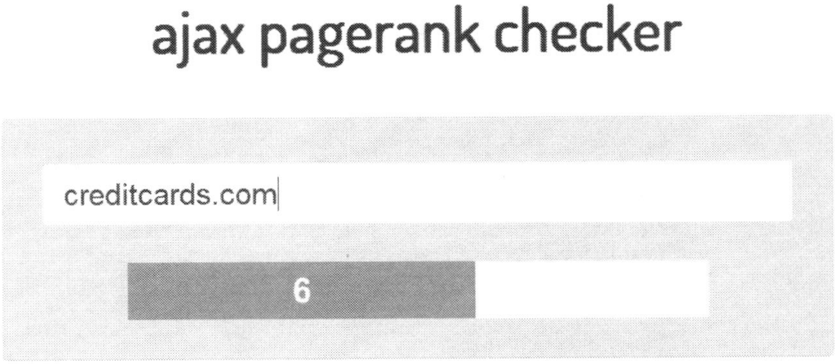

The above example shows the page rank of the domain creditcards.com at 6, which is very high.

It is important to understand that if you have a high page rank site, you have more authority. When you have more authority, the content you write on your site is considered more reliable and trusted by Google.

So if you have a website with a page rank of 4 or 5 and you want get traffic for a keyword that has little or no competition but some volume, you can write a keyword targeted article about that keyword and likely get ranked in the top spots on Google.

That is how ehow.com and about.com and those other huge "authority sites" get ranked for pretty much everything. It is because their page ranks are so high that the search engine will automatically assume that their new pages should be ranked for the corresponding keywords they are competing for.

This can be done even if the general theme of the site is not about what you are writing the keyword targeted article on. However, during the last Google Panda update (meaning algorithm update) they tried to make the Google algorithm more biased when ranking content from high page rank sites that were not relevant to the overall theme of the site itself.

So let's say that your overall site's theme is about racing cars and you have a page rank of 5. You happen to be doing keyword research on "gardening and plants" and you find out that there is a keyword related to "gardening and plants" that has decent search volume and little competition. If you try to write an article on this keyword to get it ranked on your racing cars site, Google will likely now take into account that even though you are an authority site with a high page rank, you are an authority site on racing cars, not gardens or plants.

Therefore, that last update changed how Google ranks information that is completely off-topic or out of the norm. However, sites like ehow.com and about.com just so happen to be about everything, so they were not likely affected by the update at all.

But if you found a "racing car" keyword that you hadn't ever noticed, rest assured that with a page rank of 5 on that theme, you would most likely get ranked very nicely for it.

Now that we understand why website page rank is so important, let's discover how to get your page rank up that high so that it can be at authority status. Your page rank is determined by many things, such as: how old your site is, how many "backlinks" (sites linking to your site) you have, your monthly traffic volume, and your website's overall "contribution" to our planet, among other things.

Let's take a quick look at a backlinking image:

The more websites that we get to link back to our websites, the larger influence it has on our page rank and overall likelihood of getting ranked. Getting links back from other highly ranked websites will have a bigger impact on our ability to increase our own page rank.

With that being said, a link back from a page rank site of 7 is much more significant that a page rank of 6. In the next chapter I will explain how backlinking works in much greater detail.

***

Connecting the dots

- *Your page rank report card determines the likelihood of getting ranked for new content you publish to the web.*
- *You page rank is determined by many factors, some of which are: your domain name's age, how many backlinks your site has, your traffic volume, your "contribution" to the world, and more.*

Chapter 5: On Building Backlinks

"Obtaining backlinks is much like running for president, in that he who gets the most votes will win."
~Justin A. Spencer

Building backlinks to your website is perhaps the most important part of your SEO business model. The more relevant and powerful the backlinks are that you have linking back to your website, the higher you will be ranked on the search engines for your keywords. The higher you are ranked, the more likely you are to get traffic from those keywords once your free search listing gets bumped up to the first page.

Inbound links are also a term used when discussing backlinks. Inbound links are links that are linked to your site, so for you, they are inbound or ingoing. Likewise, outbound or outgoing links are links on your site that point to other websites.

The higher the page rank is on websites that are linking to your site, the more weight the link will give your domain. Perhaps one of the best ways to get a handle on backlinks is to look at a super simple piece of html code that represents the coded side of a backlink.

When you are browsing a web page and see blue text with an underlined link on the page, it likely means that you have come across an anchor text backlink.

This is an example of an anchor text backlink. Notice how the words "anchor text" are linked back to a website. When you build backlinks back to your web page, you will want to make sure you link back your preferred keyword that you would like to rank for.

Look at it this way, there are 2 steps:

1) Linking back to your web page
2) Making sure the "anchor text" part is the keyword you want to rank for

So if your website address is called BreadisAwesome.com and you are interested in ranking for the keyword "bread," make sure when building backlinks that you link the content on other sites as such:

Here is an excellent resource on bread ingredients, the bread making process and bread in general.

To do this, you could find a relevant website to post a comment on to get a link back to your site, like BreadBakingRecipes.com for example.

So if a link to BreadisAwesome.com was published on a BreadBakingRecipes.com webpage, then BreadisAwesome.com would have just gotten a backlink from a fellow website that talks about the same topic—and if the page rank of BreadBakingRecipes.com is greater than 0 then the link will immediately add value to the BreadisAwesome.com site when Google's search spiders crawl the new backlink.

Don't worry about how to get backlinks—the purpose of this chapter is concerned with what they are. You will learn in the following chapter how to get them.

Here is what that linked text looks like on the code side:

<a href = "http://BreadisAwesome.com"> Bread </a>

The "a" stands for "anchor" as in "anchor text link", inside the carrots "<" and ">" the hypertext reference "href" is the "hypertext reference" or website address. Outside the anchor carrots is the linked content (keyword) which is *bread* in this case.

The more inbound links you have directed at your website, the more valuable and trusted your website becomes in the eye of the search engines, and your keyword rank will increase every time new backlinks leading to your site are crawled by Google's search spiders.

Anchor text variation

When you are building links back to your website or when you hire someone else to do so, make sure that you don't have the person build anchor text backlinks to your site with the same keyword for every single link.

For instance, let us pretend you found a company that can build 200 backlinks for your website for one URL (Universal Resource Locator a.k.a. your web address) and they say "you get one URL and 3 keywords".

What they mean is this: They will build 200 links to your website, and of those 200 anchor text links they can divide the links into 3 anchors or approximately 66 links for each keyword.

If your website is SoccerSportsFan.com and your main (seed) keyword is "Soccer sports apparel," then do some quick research and see if there are synonyms for this phrase that have a reasonable amount of search volume.

So you if you had 66 links per anchor keyword pointed at your site, SoccerSportsFan.com, they would look like this: (scroll over link to see the destination)

Soccer sports apparel

Soccer sports clothing

Soccer sports equipment or something like: soccer sports apparel clothing line

Remember, you can do a variation of your seed keyword, like in the 4th example. The reason for diversifying your anchor links is to tell Google's link crawling spiders that you are not spamming your links—which is to say that you are gaining credibility "naturally", by having sites link to yours for all types of related search terms.

Link diversification

The location on a website and the type of website that provides you with a backlink is another important factor. In order to make it seem like your website is being "naturally" linked to because you simply have great content that readers want to share, you need to make it appear to Google's link crawling spiders that the process looks natural.

To do this we need to focus on getting links from many different types of websites. Here is a quick list of different types of websites and different types of links you can point back to your page to make your link portfolio well-rounded.

- Blog Comments – You can get this type of link by placing a backlink to your site when commenting on a blog owner's web page.
- Forum Profiles – This type of link is acquired by joining a forum and in your profile you place a link back to your site.
- Social bookmarks – Signing up with delicious.com, reddit.com, tumblr.com and the many other social sites allow you to place a "bookmark" or social profile on the social site for your website with a link back to your website.
- Web 2.0 properties – YouTube, Squidoo, Hubpages, Wikipedia, and Craigslist are all websites that you have access to, can sign up with, and share your own content are considered web 2.0.
- Article directories – On websites like EzineArticles.com and GoArticles.com, you can submit an article with corresponding backlinks to your site.
- Blogs posts – You can place anchor text links in a blog post directing towards your site. There are blog owners who have high page ranked blogs that will do link trades/swaps/etc with you for the purposes of boosting each other's site credibility.

Avoid "link exchanges" or "reciprocal linking" which is where you and one person each place a link to each other's site which seems like a good "piggyback method", but it will backfire.

Always link to a different site that isn't linking to you if you can help it. Don't link back to sites sending you links; Google will simply think you are trying to cheat the system.

Making Sure Your Links are Crawled

When Google crawls the web, one of the things it will crawl is your backlinks. Not all of your links will be crawled (which means noticed) by Google and in turn you will not get the value of that link in that case.

There is a service you need to sign up to here: http://linklicious.me.

This service tells you which links are getting crawled by Google. If you pay others to do backlinking for you they can provide you with a report and you can compare the report they provided with Linklicious in order to determine if the sites they put your links on ever get noticed by Google.

Some pages with stale content obviously do not get indexed by Google's spiders often, unlike CNN.com for example which gets indexed daily.

So make sure you are getting what you paid for by understanding if your links are being traced to help boost your SERPS (Search Engine Results Pages).

The sandbox

Slow down, Sally! You need to learn how to walk before you can run! The same axiom holds true with linkbuilding. Do not expect Google to reward you for building 10,000 backlinks to website a week after you buy a new domain name.

Your domain name will be flagged with an invisible tracker without your awareness for spamming the web with links pointing back to your site. The algorithm Google has can recognize spam activity from natural looking activity.

What will happen if you do spam? You will be placed in something commonly referred to as "the sandbox". This means your site will not be listed on the web via Google's index for a period of time.

Obviously, it is not a permanent ban from Google's index. If it were, we would have to be very cautious and afraid of our competitors because they would be able to get our websites banned from Google if they built a million links back to our website in a day or two.

What is a safe bet? I build 200 links per month back to sites that are new. You can do more or less. If you plan on building more, then diversify where your links are coming from. Do not just have 500 links coming from the same service or company. Mix it around make sure your links are entirely different from one another—mix up the type of link and type of website the links are coming back from.

How long does the sandbox last? It will depend on a number of factors. I have had a site sandboxed for 2-3 months before and it stunk, but it wasn't the end of the world.

I made the same mistake I'm telling you not to make, which is to say I built 2,000 backlinks to a website that had a pr of 0 (meaning it was new) and it was all from the same service provider. I did not diversify the links, 90% of which were forum profile links from the same service provider.

***

Connecting the dots

- *Make sure to build variations in your anchor texts when you are engaging in link-building or when a person you hire is doing the link building for you.*
- *Diversify your links so that they do not all come from the same service provider and so that they are not all the same type of backlink.*
- *Sign up with linklicious.me to keep track of your backlinks being crawled.*
- *Do not build a large amount of links back to a new site because you can get sandboxed from Google.*

Chapter 6: Best Link Building Services

"Do your homework when looking for backlinking services, it can save you time, money, energy and just a little bit of frustration."
~Justin A. Spencer

I have tried many backlinking services throughout my experience in building SEO based marketing businesses.

Automation is essential with the SEO model in order to reach success quicker. There are many hyped-up SEO services out there you can choose from, and there are companies that will knowingly do an awful job performing search engine optimization for you. I know of but a few that are actually worth investing your money in.

I have used the following linkbuilding services:

- LinkVana – http://linkvana.com (blog postings & article postings)
- LinxBoss – http://linxboss.com (blog postings & article postings)
- Boostability – http://Boostability.com (everything—they diversify for you)
- Fiverr backlink building jobs – http://fiverr.com
- Paul's Quality Backlink Service – http://pjsqualitybacklinks.com/ (forum profile links)
- Distribute Your Articles.com – http://distributeyourarticles.com (mass article links)

- Directory Maximizer – http://directorymaximizer.com (directory based links—not article submissions—of directories that are much like "white pages", with a quick description of your business followed by your website link)

LinkVana: http://linkvana.com

LinkVana is a private blog network platform filled with multiple different categories. This was one of the first services I used when I started forming my first SEO business. One thing I did not like about LinkVana was that their service is not fully automated. You have to log into the dashboard and write a 100 word post, with included anchor text backlinks yourself.

You can outsource this part of the deal for $2 per post; however that would be extremely pricey. This equates to about $1 per link because you are limited to two links per blog post for quality purposes. The monthly cost to use the LinkVana service is $147/month. If you do not have much startup capital then I do not recommend selecting this service.

Although LinkVana is not the best choice because it requires payment without automation, the service will provide very high quality and relevant backlinks to your blog/website. When I did use their service, despite the additional work required, I did see a positive outcome from the inbound links I received from their blog network.

So all in all, they provide great quality links, but you have to do the work and still pay a hefty sum.

LinxBoss: http://linxboss.com

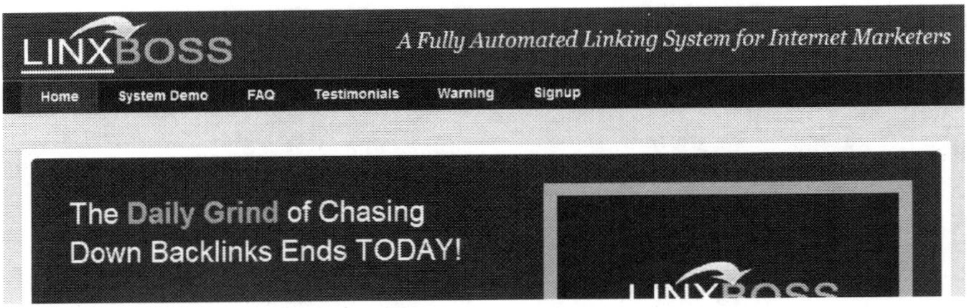

LinxBoss is my **favorite** service to date for more than a few reasons.

1. They are a fully automated backlinking service.
2. The service is owned by internet marketers, so if you have a feature request or tip or just plain out need help with something, these guys understand.
3. Value and price point: Their service is $147/month like LinkVana. However, unlike LinkVana, everything is automated. They build 200 inbound links on websites with a page rank of 1 – 6 back to your websites.
4. Additional value: You can build 200 inbound links back to 5 different websites, rotating between 3 different keywords per website.
5. Add-on options: If you want to build backlinks to more than 5 websites you can simply buy 5 more domains for an additional $97/month. The more website slots you buy from them, the cheaper the price gets. This is every internet marketer's dream. If you decide to offer SEO linkbuilding services to other online or offline businesses, you can charge your clients $200+/month for one of your LinxBoss slots. Explain to them you will give them 200 high quality backlinks for $200 – makes sense to an "offliner", right? This is a solid tradeoff for the small cost on your end ($29.40) for no work or labor.

I still use LinxBoss for my SEO based businesses today. I have 50 slots that drive a total of 10,000 backlinks back to 50 of my websites (200 links per site). The more slots you buy, the cheaper they become.

Boostability (owned by SEO.com): http://boostability.com

I have had a few positive and negative experiences with these guys. They give you two options. The first option is to pay a flat rate month to month to have their professional SEO team do backlink building, bookmarking, article submissions and blog posting for you.

These are all good SEO activities, however their professionals charge $25-35/hour. So if you're paying $100 per month there is only so much a "professional" can do for you in 3-4 hours.

So you can't expect to get nearly as much bang for your buck with that model of service if you roll with these guys. Another drawback is that there is a non-refundable $100 setup fee, plus the monthly fee you agree on charged right away. These 3-figure fees can add up quickly if you are charging everything to a credit card for you business if you do not have capital.

The second type of service they offer is SAAS, or software as a service. I will admit that I believe this service is worth it. It costs $50/month plus the $100 set up fee. What the software does for you is this: it finds relevant "do follow" blogs, directories, bookmarking sites, directory submission sites and other authority web pages for you that you can post a comment to or send a submission through to obtain relevant/quality backlinks.

The term "do follow" opposed to "no follow" refers to a link attribute. If a link attribute is set to "no follow", then the search engines with not track that link and otherwise give your site credibility from that link, so it makes the backlink pointless if is not "followed".

On my very first website, CreditCardPreference.com, I used this service and over the course of 6-7 months, the page rank became a 2. It is relatively fantastic to see results like that and I do largely believe that the Boostability software allowed me to create that type of page rank.

The obvious problem with this particular SAAS is that it is not automated at all. To be practical, this is not a bad place to start because the month-to-month cost is a fraction of LinxBoss or LinkVana, however it does require you to login and build the links yourself.

The best way to effectively leverage Boostability's SAAS would be to outsource the link building work to someone on Odesk.com or Elance.com for a conservative hourly wage.

More on outsourcing in (Chapter 13: On Outsourcing).

Fiverr.com: http://fiverr.com

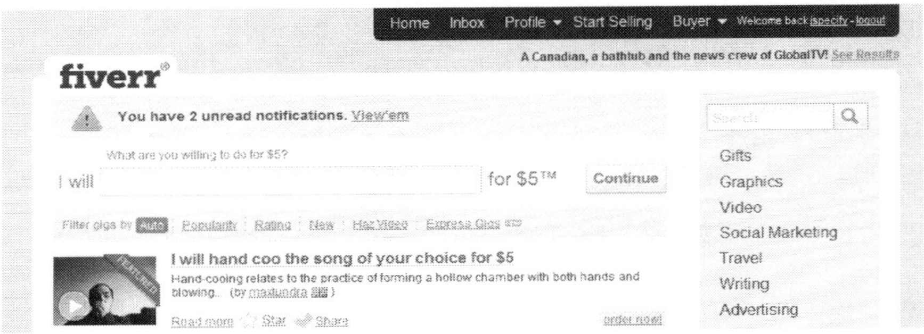

Fiverr is not only an interesting place to hire people to do backlinks for you, it is also an interesting place in general to visit to see what people are actually willing to do for $5.00. Technically, it's only $4.00 because I believe the website takes $1.00 per job.

I have hired a few different individuals on Fiverr to create .edu (domain.edu) profile backlinks towards my domains. Education and government website addresses are held in high regard with the search engines and also normally have a high page rank.

So obtaining these types of inbound links is an important part of the link building process. All in all, I would not choose to use Fiverr again in the future for a few different reasons:

1. Although the cost is low and the quality appears to be high, the phrase "you get what you pay for" tends to carry over. The Fiverr

services have been used over and over again, so the websites that are supposed to be building value and credibility towards your website are becoming link farms with low or no quality.
2. With this in mind, having low quality backlinks it just as bad if not worse than having zero backlinks. Having other crappy sites attempt to give your site credibility is a purposeless process. The name of the game is to seek high quality links.
3. A $4 investment in my book does not guarantee quality. So if I went back in time I would refrain from using the SEO services on this site.

Don't be shy in regards to the other services though! There are some extremely funny gigs on the webpage that can steal your attention for minutes or hours.

With that being said, proceed with caution if you don't want to lose your focus.

Paul's Quality Backlinking Service: http://www.pjsqualitybacklinks.com

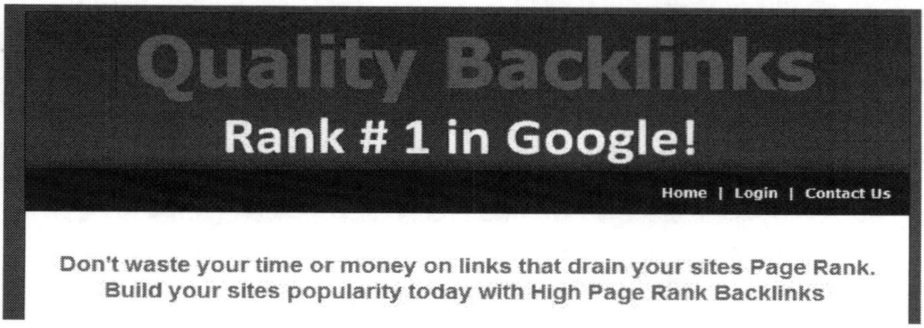

Paul's backlinking service used to be one of my favorite services until the recent Google Panda update gave ".edu profile backlinks" and otherwise "nested .edu backlinks" less credibility or "link power".

To further clarify this: A profile backlink is where you register to become a member of an organization or forum and therefore you have the ability to post a backlink or backlinks to your web page in your account/member profile.

A "nested link" is a backlink from any page that is not the homepage of a domain. So if there is a link pointing back to your site from

Website.edu/page3532.html as opposed to Website.edu, the /page edu link now carries less link power.

Homepage edu links remain extremely powerful. Inbound links from Website.edu addresses carry a lot of "link weight" and the benefit from such a link will be substantial.

Paul had/has a variety of linkbuilding services. The service I had selected was a fully automated one.

Here are the benefits of the automated service I used:

1. The price point was $174/month and this service is a great deal when you take a look at what is included.
2. With this particular SEO service, Paul and his team would drive 500 inbound high page rank .edu backlinks to four separate websites with a rotation of 3 keywords per website. (2,000 links total)

Some of websites I optimized with Paul's service ended up doing very well. One successful website even went on to get 3,000 hits per month with an average of 5,900 page requests. This particular marketing business generates $1,000.00 - $1,700.00 profit per month. More on this in (Chapter 11: Real Life Examples of Successful Sites).

However, some of the more competitive keywords I was competing for did not end up doing so well after 5-6 months of the service. I have my own speculations and theories as to why that may be, such as the Google Panda update for starters and the sandbox.

But, overall I do recommend Paul's link building services because they have assisted in the creation of one of my profitable SEO businesses.

Distribute Your Articles: http://distributeyourarticles.com

Distribute Your Articles is a platform that takes one of your articles and publishes it on multiple websites in your niche or category. This service is great for building an extremely large number of backlinks in a short amount of time. However, like the other services there are a few pros and cons:

1. One pro is that the service is not as expensive as the others; it has a price point of $50/month.
2. One con is that you are required to write articles for the distribution process and these articles have to meet specific criteria to be accepted. The articles have to be a minimum of 400 words and the content has to be original as well as legible. The main issue is that unless you enjoy writing articles, this process can be very time consuming and mentally draining.
3. If you decide to use this service and like myself, don't fancy writing content all day, then your other option is to hire someone else to write good content for you that you can use for the service. However this just racks up more costs because good content with 400+ words on average will cost $4 - $5 per article.

For example: if you want to distribute 10 articles, then the cost will be $40 - $50 plus the monthly fee. The good news is each of the articles will likely be distributed to at least 80 sites, so you can obtain potentially 80 or more links per article which will equal out to 800 links for that $60.00 assuming you put 1 link per article – Not bad right?

From a broad perspective this seems like a good deal, however the same exact article being indexed over and over again on different websites is not my idea of originality or quality. Although I was initially attracted to this way of building links I have since refrained from it.

The DYA platform did play an important part in the success of one of my online businesses, so I can assure you this method can work.

But I do not feel as strongly about distributing a single article to multiple sites to generate meaningful backlink quality. Some would argue differently, and that is fine. Feel free to experiment with this service; just know that it is not likely your best option in terms of link quality.

Directory Maximizer: http://directorymaximizer.com

Directory Maximizer was one the first backlink building services I ever used. One thing is for certain: the links they provide you with are cheap and of decent quality.

This service will submit your website to web directories for as little as $0.14 to $0.16 per directory.

On average, web directories have a page rank of 1-6, or at least they did before the most recent Panda update. Directories had their page rank values slashed by 1-2 points after the Panda update. The Panda update was intended to reward websites that have a lot of high quality content and to penalize websites that are basically just full of links without quality content (directories).

Even though directories got penalized, this does not mean they are not still worth building links back from. You can actually submit your blog to directories yourself, however paying $0.14 to $0.16 for a professional service to do it is more practical.

I used Directory Maximizer before the Google Panda update and I still will continue to use it in any future SEO business ventures.

***

Connecting the dots

- *Do your research when it comes to building backlinks.*
- *I personally recommend Linx Boss.*
- *Another great resource from someone who has used multiple backlinking services for months at a time is here: http://linkbuildingreviews.com/*

Chapter 7: The ".blogspot.com" Phenomenon

Google likes to get ranked on the first page of their own search results without following the same rules that other website owners have to follow. Some say this is okay because they own the service while others disagree.

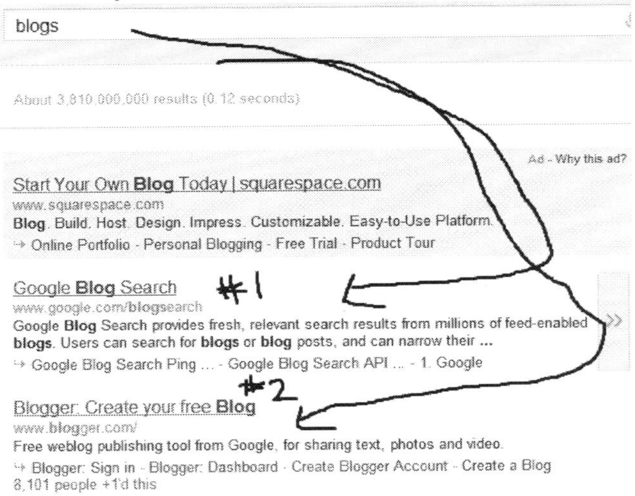

Google owns the blogger.com blogging platform also known as blogspot.com. They also own Google because they are Google, so they can decide how they want to be ranked for certain keywords while disregarding their own algorithm that everyone else has to follow. Believe me when I say that a whole book could be written about how Google doesn't follow the same rules everyone else does who uses their services—but then again this book is not about how Google is a bully or unfair.

That is not what this chapter is about—well not entirely at least. I'm merely pointing out an obvious fact; however it is related to what I like to call the ".blogspot.com" phenomenon, but this elusive phenomenon is not the fact that Google owns it; Google could offer a ridiculous price for anything they prefer to own.

It's a phenomenon for less obvious reasons. A brief investigation of ".blogspot.com" related domains can quickly inform an investigator that if you choose to blog on Google's platform you automatically are a better author, write better content, and evade the search engine algorithm discrepancies that other forms of content management systems and other methods of SEO optimization that websites typically employ.

Bold assumptions…Let us speculate further…

Disclaimer: I do not know the answers to some of these questions. I am simply asking them to stir up some thought. These are my questions:

- Do you get ranked better, and in turn receive more traffic because you are blogging on a platform owned by Google?
- Does Google potentially own the intellectual property rights to your blog's contents?
- Are they simply trying to expand their traffic empire even further by informing these bloggers how to make money with <u>their</u> ad distribution platforms and systems?

  I love innovation and I'm all about reinventing, reshaping and improving business growth for prosperity – but – let's look at the following page ranks of 3 random blogs:

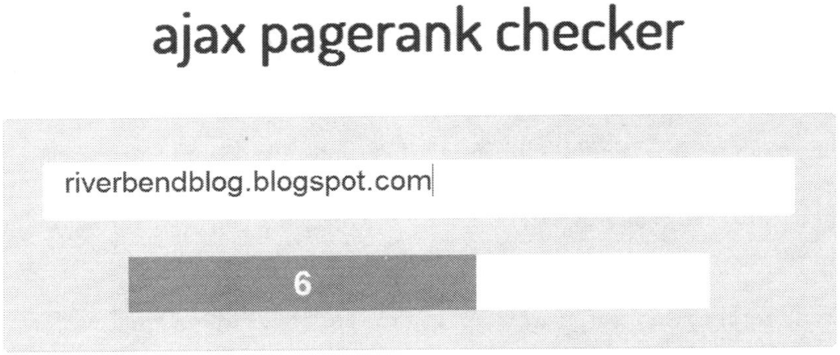
ajax pagerank checker
riverbendblog.blogspot.com
6

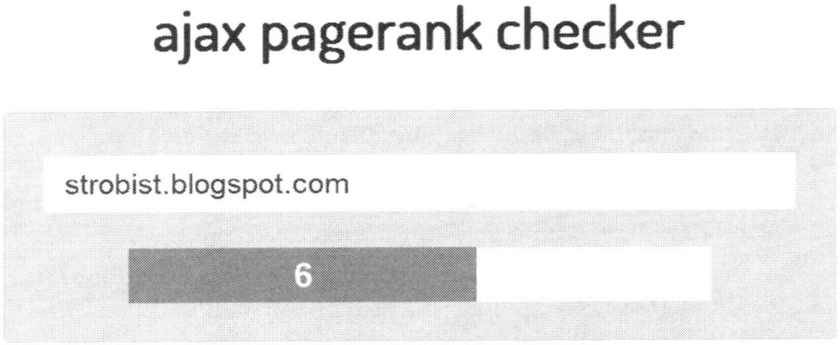
ajax pagerank checker
strobist.blogspot.com
6

ajax pagerank checker
whatkatieeate.blogspot.com
6

Everyone is now aware, that the higher your page rank is, the better your search listing ranks will be and in turn you will get more traffic and make more money.

The owners of non-".blogspot.com" websites may be at a disadvantage in terms of taking the easy road to a high page rank and in turn, a profitable business model.

My point is this:

This looks like nothing more than a deceitful way to create an extra income stream for Google. They supply free hosting and in return they give the blog owners tons of traffic which can be used in conjunction with their Ad-sense program to gain advertising revenues.

Now that we have that out in the open, another obvious fact becomes visible. Search-driven marketing businesses rely solely on Google not only to thrive, but to exist.

So how do we use Google's jacked-up Blogspot blogs to our advantage?

> Option 1) You can create your own blogs with Blogger to get traffic and make money.
> Option 2) You can get high quality backlinks from other .blogspot.com blog owners.

These blogs have an abundance of opportunities such as:

1. You can purchase advertising space – you would do this by sending the blog owner a nice email explaining you would like to put a banner ad on their website for $50.00 per month (if you are doing information/affiliate marketing).
2. Guest blog posts – you can offer to write high quality blog posts that contain backlinks for your preferred keyword back to your site.

This will not only create a traffic surge from the blog post itself, but it will also undoubtedly increase your search rank for that keyword.

How do we contact the blog owner?

Simply draft an email and send it to each of them. You can personalize each email by adding a section saying, "I really like your [category] blog" where category is equal to cooking, running, sports, cake making, etc. Also, address the email to their first name, so obviously change that with each email to add that important personal touch.

When you harness these benefits and put them into action, you will sprinkle a large impact onto your SEO driven business.

***

Connecting the dots

- *Google is likely biased towards everything they own in a positive way.*
- *You can use their bias to your advantage by 1) getting high quality backlinks from .blogspot.com blogs or 2) you can make your own .blogspot.com blogs*

Chapter 8: More Ways to Get Free Quality Backlinks

"A penny saved is a penny earned."
~Benjamin Franklin

This chapter is about getting high quality backlinks without opening your wallet. However, not spending money to get backlinks requires you to spend your time and since time has a price, you're spending a more valuable currency in my opinion.

More often than not, many individuals who find themselves entering this business are on a shoestring budget. This is perfectly acceptable. Many extremely successful internet entrepreneurs that are worth millions today got started by investing in a $9 domain name.

Obviously there's more to the process than that. They didn't pay $9 to magically make millions like paying $9 for a winning lotto ticket. But they did have an idea that added value to the masses.

But the point remains, you do not need to have tons of money to create a successful SEO driven business model. There are plenty of ways to take care of the tedious backlinking process while spending little or no money at all.

As we discussed in the previous chapter, one of the best ways to get very qualified links is to find other webmasters who have highly regarded blogs that are already ranked high in page rank. Finding these 2.0 websites that allow you to add content is your best bet.

If you have a weight loss blog, then common sense leads us to search the phrase "weight loss blogs" and/or "weight loss .blogspot.com" or "weight loss powered by Wordpress". These search phrases indicate that we are searching for highly regarded and authoritative websites that can give our website some solid credibility by allowing us to add content to them (Wordpress is a blogging platform).

The content can be in the form of a "guest post" or a simple comment—either of which will help increase the value of your own website. A guest post will obviously hold more value because you can add more than one link depending on the webmaster's conditions and how long the post is, and you can add your anchor text link surrounded by plain text.

Anchor text links surrounded by "plain" or "organic" (meaning not linked) text are given more weight because they seem natural or meant to be there. This is just another small piece of the puzzle in understanding how Google distributes backlink weight.

The above example is also called in-line links. Meaning the links are in the middle of plain text and the process has a nice flow.

The "powered by Wordpress" phrase is a familiar term that is on the bottom of some (not all) Wordpress blogs. The ".blogspot.com" phrase is more foolproof because it addresses a similarity in the domain and not text in an unhampered Wordpress footer.

Once you uncover these sites you can make a list of them and then go through them, either commenting on them, or by emailing the person asking to do a guest post (which will yield the best results).

You can link-back to your websites using other web 2.0 sites such as:

1. Craigslist
2. YouTube
3. Facebook
4. Twitter
5. Delicious
6. Reddit
7. Stumble Upon
8. Hub Pages
9. Squidoo
10. Any blog on the internet

***

Connecting the dots

- *You can get backlinks for free by investing your time instead of your money.*
- *This is a great way to go about it if you are on a shoestring budget.*
- *There are a ton of possibilities – don't limit yourself to the small list above.*

Chapter 9: On-Page Optimization

"The other 10% of your search relevancy"

"On page optimization" only yields about 10% of page ranking weight as compared to the 90% that the backlinks yield. However, that does not mean this part or phase should be overlooked.

Here is one of the best processes or flow models to follow when assigning your page with a keyword:

1) Your page name

Let's assume your domain name is WeightLossGuide.com and the keyword you are trying to gain traffic by getting ranked for is "foods that help you lose weight". This is a long tail keyword that likely has less competition. Therefore, we are more likely to get ranked and receive traffic from it.

The name of the page itself should be the keyword or the keyword with a word added only in the front or at the end of it. So the result could look like this (notice the word 'five' and 'fast' have been added):

WeightLossGuide.com/Five-**foods-that-help-you-lose-weight**-fast

The purpose of adding the words in front or back is to separate your page from the competition while still remaining relevant. Other people are likely competing for this particular phrase because they have also noticed the traffic opportunity.

Sticking out in this example is not bad idea.

2) Making good use of HTML header tags (h1, h2, h3, h4, h5, h6…)

During the page-creating process, make sure to include to include at a minimum one h1 tag. In html it looks like this:

<h1> Text goes here – Include a headline that explains what the page is about </h1>

Make sure your keyword is included inside this header tag regardless of whether or not it is a long tail or extremely broad keyword. Search engines are machines and they like hierarchical organization of page content.

Sprinkling h2 tags into the page to represent sub-topics related to the main topic will also build this hierarchical organization concept. If the page is very long and can be divided into sub-sub topics, you can employ the h3 tags and so on.

3) Adding relevant media to your page (images or video)

Adding one or two images that are the name of your keyword will have a beneficial effect on your on-page keyword relevance. Not only will the image build relevance, but you can also get additional free traffic from image searches.

For example, this particular website: http://travelwithJulianna.com receives a reasonable amount of free traffic from image searches. That traffic can still be of high quality because the web searcher is still likely to be interested in the topic at hand.

When you place an image onto your page, there are a few details that you will want to pay attention to. I think it best if we take a quick peek at the source code of an image. It will look like this:

<img src= “http://website.com/imagename23.png” alt = “your-keyword” />

The “src” attribute is the source of the image; the “alt” is the alternate text to be displayed in case a web browser has images disabled. The image name should be your keyword and the alternative text should be your keyword as well.

The next thing to do when placing an image on your page is to put a caption around it. You can place captions around your image easily with the Wordpress blogging platform. Within the caption, place a 2-3 sentence description of the image and sprinkle your keyword into that description. So if we had a picture of a plate full of food for our "foods that help lose weight" page our caption description could go a little something like this:

"Chicken and green beans are always great to eat after a workout. The protein in the chicken and the fiber provided by the beans allow your body to correctly heal and replenish. This dish makes #3 on our list because it is one of the best ***foods that*** *can* ***help you lose weight*** *fast."*

Including a video on your page can have large traffic benefits. The first way you can include a video is to simply take a relevant video off of YouTube and embed it on your web page. If you want to rename the video to your keyword and include different information inside that video such as a product or service you are promoting, you can contact the video owner and ask for permission to do so (if you did not create the video yourself). Making your own video is your best bet. Posting it on youtube and your website will have the best traffic benefits.

Alternatively, you can create your own video, which sounds intimidating but it is extremely easy. All that you have to do is either write an article yourself or have someone else write an article for you. Once this is done simply create an 8-10 page slide show using PowerPoint.

Simply do a screen capture of the slideshow and just briefly touch upon the points in the article and carry the benefits of whatever it is you are talking about in the article over towards a product.

At the end of the video you can recommend an affiliate product or service or one of your own products. Not only is this great because the additional media gives your page more relevance with Google, but you can get traffic from other people viewing your uploaded video on YouTube. This is a great way to drive more targeted traffic to your site at no cost!

4) Keyword density

Keyword density is the next important factor. Most content marketers will recommend a 3-5% keyword density per page. This translates to: use your keyword 3 to 5 times per 100 words of your article.

I **do not** go by this methodology and I do not mention my keywords that much. If my article is 600-800 words, I will have my writer mention the keyword about 5 times. It is obvious that 3-5% looks like you are spamming and it ruins the flow of the article if you have to incorporate repetitive words into it that do not need to be added to add value to the article.

Seriously, even though that method may please the search engine spiders, any human who comes to your site will have zero interest in a keyword saturated article.

Plus if your article is 800 words than that means you have to mention your keyword 24 – 40 times to fulfill the 3- 5% rate.

5) Content uniqueness

If you plagiarize or slightly modify an already existing article, chances are Google will notice and if they do, they can flag your site as “low quality”. It’s like going out on a date and forgetting the person’s name you are supposed to be meeting. It just makes a bad first impression that can be difficult to recover from—not to mention plagiarizing is not legal.

If you plan on hiring someone to write content for you, make sure you explain that the articles have to be 100% unique. Obviously, reading other content about a particular topic you know nothing about is the only way you can absorb new information to spit out a meaningful article. But with that being said, whether you are writing your content or you are outsourcing, make sure that the content produced is unique.

A good resource to use if you are wondering if anyone has stolen your content is http://copyscape.com. This website scours the internet and looks for signs of possible plagiarism or copyright theft.

If you have cold feet, or you are afraid you have excellent content and you do not want it stolen, you can always subscribe to their low cost service that claims to “monitor the world wide web” to look for duplicates of your information for you. If something worthwhile turns up, then they will alert you.

***

Connecting the dots

- *On-page optimization makes up 10% of your SEO rank for the keyword you are competing for.*
- *Making sure your text/images/captions are all flush with the keyword will make your webpage rank higher from an on page standpoint.*

Chapter 10: Most Preferable SEO CMS Platform

"What type of website should I have – what is a CMS?"

Content management systems (CMS) are simply a "server side" solution for making changes to your website. This means that you do not have to download your website files to your local computer to edit them and make changes; likewise you do not have to upload anything from your computer to your web hosting server for website updates.

Wordpress is the "no tech skills needed" blogging platform:

(Wordpress.com includes the CMS & web hosting) Hosted
(Wordpress.org includes the CMS which is FREE) Not hosted

The only difference between wordpress.com and wordpress.org is that on wordpress.com you can choose to get hosting and access to additional blog theme templates for a monthly fee—with wordpress.org you can download the Wordpress platform for free and you can install any other free Wordpress theme templates on your site for free as well.

Wordpress is one of the most popular CMS's used on the internet today. Wordpress is designed to be an interactive and ever-changing CMS blogging platform. It is extremely customizable in that you can switch themes or add plug-ins to your website as you see fit.

There has been talk that there could be a potential "footprint" in Google's algorithm that favors Wordpress blogs. Google likes the idea of "blogging" which are websites that publish fresh content daily and this is may be why Wordpress blogs rank better.

Obviously, the ".blogspot.com" domains hold the most weight, but Wordpress blogs are likely next in line. I use Wordpress for a vast majority of my marketing businesses.

I recommend the following Wordpress themes and plug-ins.

Themes:

- Genesis ($35 - $80 http://market.studiopress.com/themes)
- Socrates ($77 http://socratestheme.com)
- Kubrick (Free, name of theme is 'Default') Kubrick is a super simple Wordpress theme that is very easy to customize on the code side to install professionally-designed Website templates. I often design my websites in Adobe Photoshop and have my programmer code the PSD file and install it on the "Default" theme. http://wordpress.org/extend/themes/default

Plug-ins: (all free, aside from LinkEngine)

- Tinymce-advanced (Adds icons for styling the text on your pages, posts and more. It allows you to easily change font size, color, style etc.)
- Wassup (Tracks visitors that land on your website and incoming links)
- Hide-Post (You can choose to hide posts from certain parts of the blog)
- LinkEngine ($79 - Manage links across your site and cloak outgoing links; you can conceal a page or re-direct traffic to a page based on their IP address or user-agent information: http://linkengine.com more on this later…)
- Custom Permalinks (Easily change the page and post naming structures on your site such as: www.MyWebsite.com/My-Custom-Link-Structure-Name)
- Statcounter (Plug-in goes with that Statcounter.com visitor tracking software)

- Theme switcher (Allows you to switch themes between different website visitors to test different theme conversion rates, more on this later…)
- All-in-One SEO Pack (Allows you to easily manage your SEO settings for your homepage, as well as any other post or page you publish)
- Backupbuddy (Backs up the materials on your blog in case you accidentally delete the information from your server—to prevent data loss)
- Google Sitemap Generator (Automatically generates a sitemap and alerts the search engines whenever you publish new content to your site)

This is a screenshot of the inside control panel of a Wordpress website:

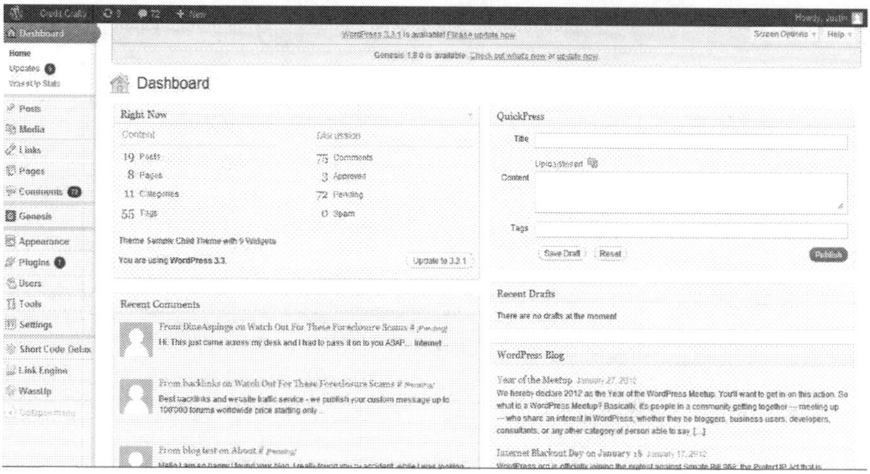

***

Connecting the dots

- *Wordpress is a great free blogging platform you can install on your websites.*

- *I use Wordpress for 95% of my marketing businesses because it is very easy to manage each website and the Wordpress blogs tend to get ranked easier for SEO purposes.*
- *There are thousands of free Wordpress theme templates you can instantly choose to install on your website, right from the dashboard shown above.*
- *There are many plug-ins you can use to further enhance your blogs customizability.*

Chapter 11: Real Life Examples of Successful Sites

"Learning by doing can be done by first seeing what needs to be done."
~Justin A. Spencer

This chapter is intended to be a treat to you. I will reveal some of my lucrative marketing businesses to you and explain the marketing aspects I use on each website.

http://SixFigureProgramScam.net - $1,500.00/mo profit website

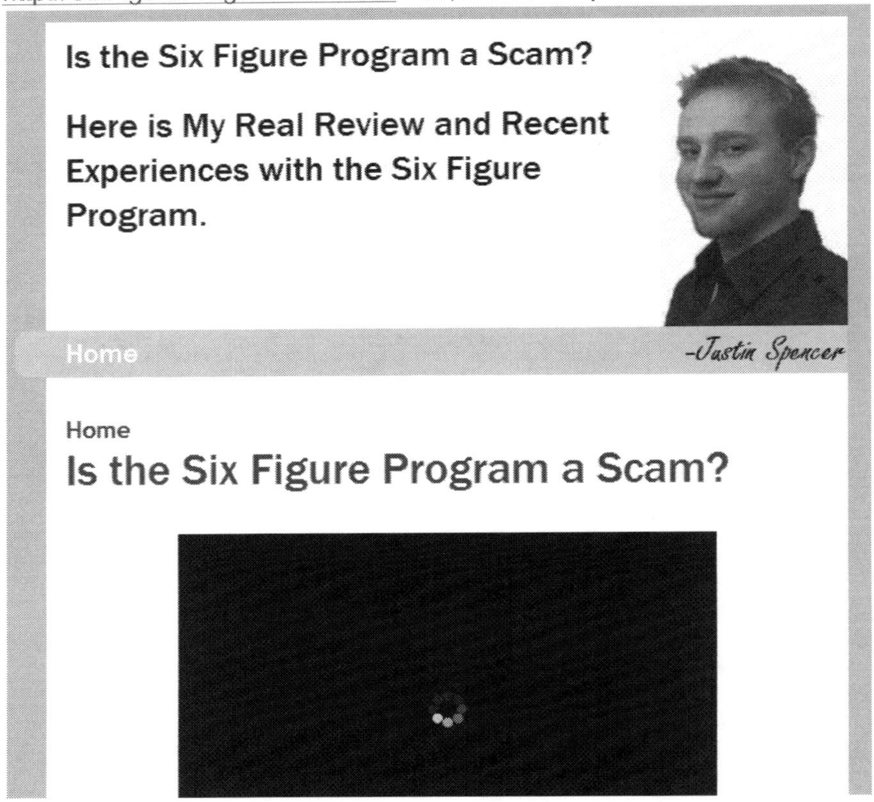

The purpose of the above pictured website is to give an honest review of a product that teaches you some key aspects in affiliate/internet marketing. I shot a quick video giving a legitimate review of the program.

Notice I followed The SEO Formula we discussed in earlier chapters—see the screenshot below:

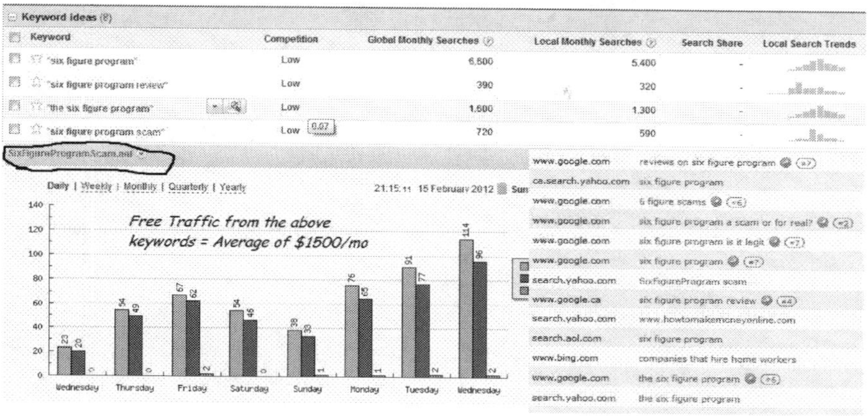

The stats are from StatCounter. More on this in (Chapter 23: On Tracking).

Let's talk about the Wordpress blog screenshot of the website pictured. On the website, I have a simple sales video I shot in about 1 hour. It took about another 1 hour to edit the video using Windows Movie Maker which is free software that comes with your PC if you have Windows 7.

I have my keyword in the top headline and in the domain name: "Six figure program scam".

Under the sales video (not pictured), I have some pictures and proof as well as a super watered-down version of my story about how I found "the six figure program" and learned some great stuff.

The purpose of the six figure program is to teach you the fundamentals of marketing and the purpose of my page is to simply send interested customers to their page as an affiliate. So I get paid for each referral that turns into a sale.

Let's look at another successful affiliate based business: http://lexingtonlawscam.org this site makes $300 - $600 per month profit.

Are The Lexington Law Scam Claims True?

I Signed Up A Month Ago With Lexington - Here is What Happened.

Lexington Law Scam - My Results

Hello! My Name is Casey and I Hired the Lexington Law Firm to Delete My Credit, Please Read My Page to Learn About My Results!

I used to have really bad credit because I mismanaged my credit card debts when I was younger.

I had a steady job, but the money I brought in did not cover the costs of my climbing credit card debt. I did not anticipate unexpected expenses like car repairs, but they were a priority and they needed to be paid.

As a result of my cumulative credit card build up my debts ended up getting charged off by my credit card companies and sold too collection agencies.

This was pretty much a nightmare because these debt agencies sent me nasty, scary letters and they would call me more than once a day. I did not know how to make them go away and my stress levels were quickly going through the roof.

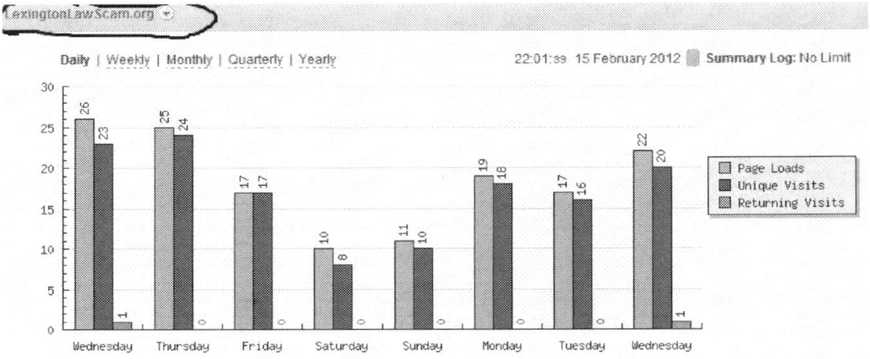

The purpose of this website is to take someone who thinks the Lexington Law Credit Repair Program is a scam and to reassure them with a positive customer experience that the service is not a scam, and that the service works quite well.

You can apply to be in the Lexington law affiliate program through http://cj.com or http://www.progrexion.com/online-affiliate-home.

***

Connecting the dots

- *The SEO formula works. I have over 100 websites as of 2/15/2012. If those two affiliate businesses are doing almost $2,000/mo—then yes—100 websites…you can do the math, it adds up.*
- *When creating affiliate landing pages, the idea is to keep it simple.*
- *My websites do not look spectacular but they get traffic and that traffic turns into money. Period.*
- *Scaling the SEO formula alone can change your entire lifestyle.*

Chapter 12: Rinse Before You Repeat

"Dip your foot into the pond, before you jump in"
~Justin A. Spencer

Like most SEO-driven marketing business owners, you will likely assume that you have uncovered an unscathed keyword or set of keywords that constitute as "hidden gems" or "gold nuggets".

Before you get excited and buy 15 domain names, make sure that the keywords meet the criteria for being profitable and make sure you understand that you may be dropping $150 like it's hot on domain names that may not produce a profit.

Before you buy all of the keyword-rich domains that clutter your registrar account, you need to do a quick reality check—I like to call this "rinsing" as opposed to "repeating". I'm implying that you should test two or three of the domains by doing standard procedure.

Host the domains, install Wordpress, put the domain addresses into your link-building funnel, add some content, install proper tracking and then wait about 4 weeks.

If you start actually getting a few unique hits each day for the keyword then you can now assume that the investment has the potential to be a profitable business. There are not many things in this business more annoying than having 91 spare or unused domains in your registrar account.

Once you recognize that you have 2-3 blogs that are generating traffic which have the potential to be transformed into money, then lean forward and replicate this process.

***

Connecting the dots

- *Make sure what you are investing your money in shows promise before getting carried away and making a sizeable investment.*
- *Lower your financial risk before investing in anything.*
- *Use common sense.*

Chapter 13: On Outsourcing

"Surround yourself with the best people you can find, delegate authority, and don't interfere as long as the policy you've decided upon is being carried out."

~Ronald Reagan

Being transparent when outsourcing projects

Outsourcing can either be your friend or your enemy. There are a few very important things you should know before hiring employees to fulfill simple maintenance and tasks and/or bigger, more important projects such as website design or development.

The most vital component for successfully outsourcing is to be as transparent as possible with your contractors. When you communicate with your subcontractor or employee, you have to be as specific as if you are talking to a kindergartner. This concept does not have boundaries. Meaning, if your contractor is in the United States or India, the same concept applies.

The first time you try to communicate something that seems to be "common sense" or "common knowledge" with someone you have hired, will be the first time you realize how amazingly different people interpret things.

Outsourcing is like a secret weapon if you use it properly. It can also backfire because work that is done to the wrong specifications or with poor quality often creates a mess that needs to be cleaned up by the contractor or more often than not, you. So if you are paying someone to perform a service for you, make sure the job is done right.

Let me give you an example: I hired someone from a particular country outside the U.S. to do some graphic design work. This person had a decent portfolio with solid credentials and it appeared as if they had been in the logo and graphic design scene for a while.

I wrote a brief description of how I had imagined the logo and site design to look and I gave a few examples of other websites to allow him to see the direction I was leaning towards.

To make a long story short, the project should have taken 2-3 days and after about 2 weeks, 3 different site designs and about 16 revisions later, I finally realized that I was throwing broken darts at a dartboard 2 miles away.

I just could not find the right combination of words to communicate or portray my visualization to this person. Obviously, I could have been far more specific and descriptive in the beginning which could have influenced how the contractor had visualized this particular graphic design project.

My sense of clarity and this person's sense of clarity were as close to opposites as mentally possible when communicating how a site design should look. So the project was over before it started. I paid the person for the crappy designs and I did not bother downloading them. I had learned a valuable lesson.

Before hiring someone else to do this project, I took 45 minutes and wrote down every possible thing about this project I could possibly think of. After this brainstorming session, the project was explained in such a detailed manner that I was certain the next contractor I hired would be able to grasp my vision with little or no clarification.

Sure enough, the next person who designed my site absolutely blew me away; it looked even better than I had imagined and the only revisions that were necessary were simple shifts or movements in the headline and sidebar for marketing purposes.

Fact: Being transparent upfront will save you valuable time and money.

When I hire individuals to perform repetitive tasks, I do not even bother writing a description of what needs to be done. For these types of cases I shoot a 15-20 minute video covering every detail of what needs to be done, while demonstrating what it is I want to be done and how it needs to be done, all captured on video. This reduces the chances of confusion to about 1%.

Knowing when to outsource

Knowing when to outsource is less obvious than most realize. Some individuals feel the need to do everything by themselves. If you find yourself in that group you have to escape! Snap out of it!

Now is the time to realize that successful marketing businesses are not created by one person. If you are ambitious and you try to tackle every obstacle on your own, chances are you are going to get burned out.

Notice I said successful marketing businesses "are not created" by one person, in most cases with respect to a few anomalies. However "running your businesses" may or may not require an extra set of hands. This will vary based on the nature of your website.

If your website religiously cranks out passive income (continuous income made with little or no interference) then chances are you will not need to hire someone to help you maintain the site—unless you are looking to expand it or add extra products and/or services or if you are looking to create a new site design, etc.

Having a polished team on your side will empower you to accomplish projects in a very short amount of time. If you find yourself doing tedious tasks day in and day out on insignificant things, then it is time to outsource. When you outsource, it allows you to use your time to focus on more important things, such as project creation and marketing.

Here is a list of sites you can use to outsource (most popular from top to bottom):

1. http://elance.com
2. http://odesk.com
3. http://www.vworker.com

4. http://freelancer.com
5. http://hiremymom.com

Creating your empire

Imagine that you have an idea that you want to become tangible, for example, say you wake up with an uncontrollable urge to be a dominant competitor in the weight loss industry. You have an idea for an app, a book, an exercise kit, a diet kit or some type of product or service related to losing weight. With an able team at your side you can delegate all of the tasks necessary to allow your product or service to take shape.

There are many elements involved with creating and launching a product. Attempting to do every task by yourself is impractical. A typical product launch includes: writing a sales letter, creating a sales video, creating the web page graphics, developing a product launch strategy, developing a promotional strategy, gathering affiliates and the list goes on and on.

***

Connecting the dots

- *Be transparent when communicating with your subcontractors/employees. You can do this by being specific, detail oriented and by communicating in a 3rd grade type of communication.*
- *Know when you need to outsource. If you are making great progress and realize you always come to a screeching halt when you get to a particular part of your project, then you need to hire someone who has the proper skill set to fill your void to keep moving forward.*
- *It is not only impractical, but plain stupid to try and execute an idea by yourself. Successful people work smarter, not harder. If you find yourself in a position to execute a great idea, hire great people to help, and you will get great results.*
- *Remember, work smarter, not harder. It is much SMARTER to surround yourself with other competent people that can help you achieve your goals.*

Chapter 14: Creating an Authority SEO Model Marketing Business

"Successfully creating an authority-based website is like successfully developing and leasing an apartment complex—the money just keeping coming in."

Distinguishing between planning, designing and doing

This section is dedicated specifically to the process behind planning, designing and implementing the creation of an "authority" website. There is a different process involved when you choose to go this route and there are many important features that you have to be aware of.

The key difference between the "authority model" and other SEO business models discussed in this book is that the other strategies involve less time and risk to implement.

Instead of creating an SEO based business to rank around one or a few sets of keyword phrases that have lower competition, the authority model seeks to rank for a broader range of keywords that have high competition and higher value.

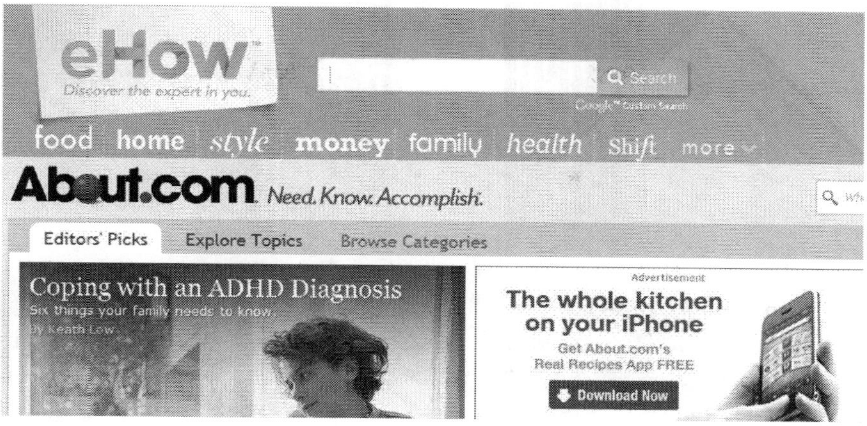

Ehow.com and about.com are great examples of authority sites – these two sites literally talk about everything and have 1000's of web pages relevant to many different categories.

You do not need to specialize in every single category to be an authority site. You can be an authority on one single topic like: finance, or business, or weight loss.

Domain name and registry rental period

When choosing a domain name for an authority model there are a few things to consider. Picking a website address that is unique and easy to remember which is also relevant to your category of choice will work well. Since you do not have to focus so intently on having a keyword rich domain, you have fewer limitations for being creative.

One other option you will have is to choose how long you would like to rent the domain for when you initially register it. Google has access to domain registrar information and there has been speculation that buying a domain for 8-10 years right off the bat instead of 1 year period yields some positive effect on the search rankings, because this conveys the idea that you are serious and are here to stay, therefore you should be rewarded or ranked higher accordingly.

It's like pledging allegiance to the domain you have invested in. It is very possible that Google extracts some type of bonus trust from this gesture.

Long term link-building strategy

You should have a few automated link-building solutions on hand that will take care and manage your linkbuilding campaigns for you. One classic method for obtaining proven backlinks is to simply take a peek at your competitor's backlinks.

You can do this a few different ways:

1. Go to google.com and type links:domain.com without a space between links: and the start of the domain. This will reveal any sites linking into the specified website.
2. Yahoo used to have a tool called "Yahoo Site Explorer" that showed sites linking to the specified website. They recently took down this tool and are planning to recreate it within a new set of webmaster tools, available here: http://www.bing.com/toolbox/webmaster.

Using a combination of multiple link-back (link-building) services is the best way to make sure your website's page rank gets upgraded. By diversifying where your links are coming from and starting off slow and working your way up towards more links, your site will begin to catch some momentum.

The same strategies in (Chapter 6: On Building Backlinks) still apply.

Content creation

Writing lengthy and valuable information is one of the toughest tasks when building an authority website. All authority websites that receive tons of traffic have well-written quality content that helps the web searcher fix a problem or learn more about whatever it is they are searching for.

Website development can easily be outsourced or you can install a CMS platform such as Wordpress. The content creation aspect itself seems to be the biggest obstacle for creating a successful authority site.

If you enjoy writing and you know you can commit to writing large amounts of good content consistently, then the best option for you is to simply write the content yourself. Skilled writers are not a dime a dozen. Enthusiastic writers are a dime a dozen. Most writers are not afraid to write good quality content for short intervals of time.

But there is always a plateau that is reached and the writer often becomes burnt out or starts producing stale content to "fill in the gaps". Unless you are extremely enthusiastic and you are willing to be creative every single day for a long time, you should consider hiring a few writers.

You do not need to hire half a dozen writers right away. You should hire at least one person to help supplement the content on the website if you decide to go the authority website route.

Yes, this is a large financial investment, as well as a significant time investment. In order to make sure that you get the biggest bang for your buck when you hire writers, you have to understand your options.

Someone new to this would 9 times out of 10 hire a writer or writers and simply pay them for each article. This is fine, but I have done this in the past and it has allowed me to realize just how risky starting an authority site is in terms of outsourcing costs.

When you hire a staff to supplement the content on your site, your payment terms are only limited by your creativeness. What does that mean? I simply mean that there are different ways to get free high quality content.

There is one method that will attract writers who are opportunists and see the big picture. This method will also filter out 95% of other writers who do not share the enthusiasm you desire.

The power of revenue sharing and forming partnerships

The method is this: You can hire a staff and base their contributions on a scale where they get paid a commission or (percentage) of the revenues the website produces. When you hire your writer or writers, just make sure the conditions of the deal are crystal clear.

This is substantial way to minimize your risk, financially and time-wise.

For this type of revenue sharing model, the writers would be expected to write content for the site. You, the conductor and visionary would take care of the other bells and whistles. This would mean you would front the costs for the website design, any programming that will need to take place, hosting fees and site maintenance. Also make it clear that you will pay for any necessary costs associated with site improvement, updates, or upgrades in the future. This gives you a ton of leverage and it actually seems very low-risk to the content writers as well.

This method allows the team to work *with* you instead of *for* you. When the business becomes profitable, you simply share a portion of the revenues with the writing team or the writer(s) responsible for supplying the content.

This may seem difficult to convince someone to "work for free" or "work until profitable", but in retrospective it is really not. You simply have to shove the benefits of this model into their skull and eventually you will find people who get the picture.

Here is how that is done

Now that we understand this model, let's take a look at what benefits the writer, since we have to sell our business structure to them so they will work with us.

First of all, after you read this book you will have given yourself an above average education on creating profitable marketing businesses. Completion of this book and understanding its materials will have positioned you to pronounce yourself an expert in internet entrepreneurship.

Regardless of whether you have 12 or 0 profitable online businesses, it does not matter. It is better to be a man (or woman) who has the proper skills and then takes action than simply taking action and learning the skills from the mistakes along the way that could have been bypassed.

You can position yourself in your sales pitch to your writers as an expert in creating profitable online businesses out of thin air. This way they have respect for your words on a much higher level.

If they beckon to see your businesses, you can gently explain to them that you are not here to supply proof—and that you know what you are talking about. You are here to hire ambitious writers who want a share of the profits of the next business venture you are setting your sights on.

If you get up a couple of websites up—regardless of whether they are profitable or not— you can also use those websites as proof and ammunition.

After you apply this type of directness to your team of potential subcontractors, one of two things will happen.

1. They will gain even more respect for you and their enthusiasm for working with you will increase as well.
2. They will get frustrated by the power of your authoritative words and will run back home seeking the warm comfort of a low-paying freelancing position somewhere else.

As the leader of your business, you are responsible for defining the vision. You have to see your business for what it can be, and you have to take all of your minions by the hand and show them the light. Help them harness their talents to make you and them a profitable business.

Keep in mind, that since you own the rights to the domain name, you own the site. You own anything they place on the site. You can choose to distribute ownership shares of the site if you would like, should you ever decide to sell out. This way the writers you are working with get a share of the liquidation revenues.

Obviously, it is more ethical to have this in place in the original deal and it will only help solidify the trust between you and your team by providing them with a deeper sense of security.

Now it's time for the "sales pitch" to attract enthusiastic writers to the revenue sharing model. Here are a few benefits for the writers in this business model that you can use to flare up their emotions, uncover their ambitions and harvest the writing talent they possess:

1) They get a stable, residual, reoccurring paycheck for the profits the site produces month after month. This is like candy for any freelance writer who is struggling to find work. So much writing talent goes to waste because these writers simply cannot find people like you.

Trust me; I have been a "saving grace" for a few freelancers I have hired for the long term. What do I mean by "saving grace"? One gifted freelancer was one month away from being evicted until I hired him and saved him from moving back home into his parent's basement. Believe me when I say, people will buy your ideas.

2) When selling this idea, mention websites like about.com, ehow.com, or any other relevant websites that are related to the site you are creating that are already successfully producing 5 to 6 figures per month. This will make their ears perk up like a cold breeze in the winter.

3) Freelance writers are some of the hardest working and lowest paid workers you will ever meet. It is not easy to sit down and write hundreds of pages of great content per week to make an incredibly small amount of money. Make sure to give figures and numbers in your pitch. Explain to the potential writers that you are willing to start them at 15% of the site's revenues with a possible fluctuation of 10% or more varying on the scale of their contribution to the site's success.

4) Explain to them that not "if" but "when" the site starts producing $10,000 a month, they will be entitled to 15% of those revenues ($1,500) each month for simply writing content on the site.

Then seal the deal by gently suggesting that "when" the site starts producing $100,000 per month…the attractiveness of this deal will tickle their feet and have their mind spinning.

5) Remember that you, the leader who is authoring and conducting this deal must remain the visionary; you cannot let a single shroud of doubt about your business enter your mind.

You have to be actively chasing it. You cannot wake up one day and decide to call it off or get cold feet or start having doubts. If you let yourself down on the vision or the dream, you let everyone down.

6) This business model reinforces your ability to stay motivated because you have now put the pressure on yourself. Your team is depending on your leadership to fuel the business and help their contributions create income.

With this being said, this business model is not for you if:

1. You often find yourself constantly doubting your abilities to create a profitable business. If this is you, you'll benefit from reading (Chapter 33: On Habits), to eliminate your negative thoughts.
2. You are the type of person that needs "instant gratification". This model is specifically for individuals who can stand the test of time to create something magnificent. Remember, Rome was not built in a day.

Conducting, managing, and leading your team to success

In order to properly guide your team to create this successful business, you need to make sure you know how to generate traffic with the SEO process. Reading this book should give you a pristine understanding of how the search engines reward sites with high popularity and trust by delivering streams of residual traffic.

In order to make sure that your writers are not writing about what they *think* will bring traffic, you need to take the time to do the research for the topics that need to be written about in order to create actual traffic flow and revenues. You can also choose to get a researcher in on the business deal or you can pay them separately—or you can do the research yourself.

I shot a 30 minute detail-oriented video to teach the person I hired as my researcher. She does a great job every time and it saves me tons of time having to do the research and I know I can trust her—because I taught her.

Since it is your job to find out which keywords you can get traffic from, you need to make sure you echo the criteria of the articles to your writers. Once the content starts producing traffic flow, your business will now start to create a steady flow of momentum. This will not only encourage your writers because they will know that their efforts are paying off, but more importantly this traffic has the ability to start creating revenues almost automatically.

Remember, the key is to make sure the articles are structured properly and based on the correct research that you have done or that your researcher has done for you.

Next you have to use your deductive powers like Sherlock Holmes, which is fun! After you find a list of 10 keywords you can rightfully assume will create traffic flow, you then have to inspect each keyword. I will normally write 5-6 ideas or angles to form content around that one keyword before I pass it on to my team of writers.

Obviously it seems less difficult with a broad keyword; opposed to a long-tail keyword (more than 4 words in the search query) but only if you choose to see it that way. I have convinced myself that I'm limited only by my personal creativeness, and you are well on your way to doing the same by reading and digesting the information in this book.

Let us dissect, digest, develop, discern, devalue, dictate, disassemble, dematerialize, demobilize, digress away from my spewing of words that start with a D that are all related—or are they?

Cool huh? This demonstrates that imagination has no limits. I thought of those words in 10-12 seconds because they all lead me further up the cave to the light of the topic I'm conveying to you—and I'm jacked up on Starbucks coffee right now.

This woman next to me is actually sweeping rather loudly which is threatening to disable my serene focus, but anyway...

We now know this:

1. You have your keyword that you know will generate traffic flow.
2. You now need to dissect it and process it—what does this keyword mean to you?
3. For this example, the keyword will be "how to lose weight on a budget"

Do you agree that this is a long tail keyword? Good, because it is. It is greater than four words. Now, how do we develop creative angles and ideas for our writers to write about this topic or keyword to generate traffic flow to our website?

Here is what comes to mind when I look at the above keyword:

1. This search implies that this person does not want to go to the gym or invest in weight loss apparel or gear because they are on a budget.
2. This person could be unemployed or low on money, living paycheck to paycheck.
3. This person does not have much time to work out because they are working so much to pay off their debts and living expenses.
4. This person could possibly be depressed or upset that he/she is overweight. We can use this to flirt with their emotions to gain loyal readership to our site. Since loyal = residual = more consistent money, this is referred to as creating a maximization of revenue from one user.
5. This person is likely self-conscious about how they look and they want to make a change.

6. It possible that they are outside of one of the social circles they wish to be in.
7. It is possible she/he cannot win the heart of the co-worker they work with because they are not confident due to their weight problem.
8. This person wants to know how to lose weight, she/he is not implying she/he wants to buy anything, only implying that she/he seeks information
9. I can assume this web searcher is a female because logic and experience dictate that women are more self-conscious about their body types more often than men.
10. I can affirm this person is between the age of 20 – 35, as statistics allow me to deduce this since women are most active in this phase of their life.

See how I quickly and easily deduced 10 facts about a web searcher in about 60 seconds off of little information? Now imagine we try to sell this person something and they land on our web page that has one of these headlines:

- "Who Else Wants to Lose Weight, Become More Confident and Win the Man of Your Dreams—While Spending Only $3?"
- "Who Else Wants to Chisel Those Thighs, Hips and Legs without Going to the Gym or Opening Your Purse?"
- "Who Else Wants to Trim their Waist and Tone their Legs, Butt and Thighs, Even If You are Living on a Budget?"

"Who Else" implies that others have used your advice successfully already. This will build trust and have a strong likelihood of capturing their complete attention.

My friend, those web page headlines will seem more like a dream come true than a bargain. If you know your web searcher, then you have much more control over them. That headline will likely work very well based on my brief deductions.

The content that follows would convey the ideas promised within the headline. This example was intended to be an exercise for deducing things about your keyword and market; however there are so many opportunities to monetize off of your content if you know who you are writing to.

You can even sprinkle "content-lockers" on some of your site's web pages. What content lockers do is give the searcher trying to access the web page a glimpse of the content and then it becomes "locked" until the person does a specified action, which could be to "opt-in in to your emailing list" or "to fill out a survey" to unlock the content they are trying to access. Blam Ads is a content locking gateway—check them out sometime.

You may be wondering: "But Justin, what if a male web searcher feels left out because the headline is more personal and exclusive to a female audience?"

1. Ironically, some of male searchers will likely find it funny and continue reading it anyway.
2. We know that a larger percentage of our web searchers are female, so it makes much more sense to actively engage our target audience then to target everyone.

Look at it this way: If you have 100 web searches that find your page, let's say 80 are female and 20 are men. Now imagine that you have a headline that "appeases" both genders. Now you have lost the attention to a few degrees of 80% of your audience to gain a percentage of the remaining 20% that are males.

Would you rather have the complete attention of 80% of your web searches or would you rather have the partial attention of some of your female and some of your male audiences?

I will stick to fully appeasing the bigger section of my audience.

So to summarize this section, it is your responsibility to do the keyword research or train someone to do research very well, and to make deductions about the keyword that capture your traffic source's attention to stay on the site and fulfill an action, even if your objective is to simply gain site readership.

Once you have these angles and ideas knocked out with your lists of extensive keywords, the next step is to deliver this information to your team.

After they write the articles based on your deductions of what has a great chance of working and connecting with your target audience, you will be able to know if you "hit the nail right on the head" so to say.

You can determine that by using Google Analytics to analyze how long particular pages on your site were viewed for and how they found that particular page to begin with, among many other types of information you can discern from viewing your analytics data.

It is also your responsibility to read the content and suggest changes, updates or recognize if the articles fail the task at hand. Even if you make it easy for the writers by giving them ten insights to refer to when writing their articles, humans are human. They can get tired, zone out and start getting off target by writing about nonsense that is not objective writing. It is your duty to notice this and to point it out to your team so that they know they need to fix it and prevent getting off topic when they publish to the site.

Determine monetization methods with the website

Once you start gaining traction and you have a measurable amount of traffic flow on your site, it then becomes time to determine how you would like to monetize the site. There are a million ways to earn revenues with a website.

You can refer product sales to other businesses, you can refer service sign ups to other businesses, you can generate ad revenues from a simple text or image advertisement "click- through", you can sell advertisement space, you can sell backlinks, you can sell your own products or services…the sky is the limit. Let's explore some of these further.

1) Referring product sales & referring service sign-ups (affiliate marketing)

We mentioned before that this is referred to as "affiliate marketing" or "selling other peoples stuff". This revenue generation model has its benefits and limitations. The obvious benefit is that you do not have to create a product or service. You can simply slap a referral tracking link on your web pages.

Affiliate marketing is a lucrative business model. But the profitability of an affiliate business has extreme limitations based on scalability and magnitude.

Everyone is aware that if you refer, let's say, 3 service sign ups or 3 product sales a day where you get paid $75.00 for the sale, then on average you will make $225.00 a day, which is $6,750.00 per month which is $81,000.00 per year.

Sounds easy right? Nope it's not easy, at all.

"Aha! I knew it wasn't just me! I knew that this affiliate marketing thing was really hard and not as easy as the Guru's proclaiming it to be!"

Does this sound like you? Don't be embarrassed if it does sound like you because most people who learn about affiliate marketing are fed the nonsense that it is really easy.

Does selling anything in general sound easy to you? That is what affiliate marketing is—you are simply selling other people's stuff for them. Or in other words, you are doing a lot of hard work and heavy lifting to get paid part of what the product owner (producer) earns in their bank statement.

"Wait it a minute, what? The producer is making more money than me? I'm selling his stuff!!! I'm the one building web pages, losing money on traffic and split testing headlines to try and sell his stuff – How come I make way less than him?!"

You make less than him because he has the power to scale his product or service. He has tons of hard-working affiliates doing all of the work for him. There is no risk to him if you lose money on paid traffic sources or time spent on SEO campaigns that fail.

To make matters worse, the affiliate program owner (producer) can control how much he wants to pay you for each of the sales. He/she is making the real money because their product is likely being sold by a multitude of affiliates if it is a popular product.

So if you finally do find the magical combination of sales copy, keywords and text ads that lead to a profitable campaign after all of your hard work, the product owner can decide to pay you $5 per sale because he wants to increase his margins. This can tip your campaign into the red.

This doesn't mean that product owners are unwilling to work with you to keep receiving sales, it simply outlines the limited amount of control you have over things you do not own.

One solution is to sell a similar product or service in the same industry, if your old product offer is no longer available or they are unwilling to work with you. The problem is the product or service may not yield the same amount of sales because a limitless number of variables have been changed.

The new business that you are sending customers to have a different sales process that could be better or inferior to the last offer you were marketing. The new company or offer could be incompetent at closing sales, or converting your leads into sales.

If this is the case, all hope is not lost, however you can expect to make some changes in your sales process to alleviate the changes.

Which brings you back to square one: do you really want to have to change your entire sales flow to compensate for a different yet related product in the industry you were selling for?

Unless you select a company that has a service or product that solves a common or re-occurring problem, then you can expect that your profit pipes will be turned off when you least expect it.

2) Selling your own products or services (info. marketing)

This is the most preferable business model for making money because it gives us true business ownership and control. When you sell your own stuff, you have complete control over everything, even the little things like your product or service distribution model.

Creating a product is 20% of the battle; the means in which you distribute that product is the other 80%. The greatest underexposed products in the world will never create an impact on people's lives and will therefore never create an impact on your wealth.

You can create your own products or have them outsourced. Alternatively, you can create some aspects of your product while leaving some other aspects outsourced.

The real benefit of this model is that you have control, and with that control you have the ability to scale your product. There are many ways you can do this and an affiliate program is certainly one of the best. Recruiting affiliates who to promote your products and services for you will not be hard if you have a product that addresses a need or solves a common problem that a large group of people have.

Products like this almost sell themselves, and affiliates will be inclined to send you business because they know they can profit from your product or service. Affiliates are the ultimate weapon to achieving true success because they enhance your scale or your reach and your product gets sold a lot more.

There are some one-hit wonders that have created simple e-books on Dieting and Weight Loss, or even addressing things that aren't actually problems like Learning How to Jump Higher, that sell religiously.

If you have a $17 dollar e-book, a few sales every now and then is not going to change your lifestyle. If you have affiliates sending you 50-100 sales a day, every day, you can rest assured that your standard of living will increase, dramatically.

3) Installing a code snippet to generate ad revenues (Selling ad space)

This tactic for generating income is easy to set up and that is about the only benefit. Trying to make money with ad revenue programs like Google Adsense or the Yahoo Publisher Network is an uphill battle. Unless you already have a website with tons of traffic, you will not see any life altering changes using this model.

This does not mean it is not a lucrative opportunity though. Creating traffic is the hardest part of creating any successful marketing business. If or "when" you are able to create large pools of traffic (preferably free traffic) then this model will work well.

There are some individuals who own more than 450+ niche based websites who implement this model across all of their sites. Scaling this model to the point that it can create a life-altering income like $50,000-$60,000 per month is possible.

I have not had the pleasure of meeting these two people that have done just this—Ryan Eagle and Courtney Lee— I have had a chance to speak with Courtney over the phone and I have shared emails with Ryan a few times. I have not met them in person and as you can imagine they are extremely busy—and I'm no slouch either.

However, the amount of work involved is ungodly. You will need a team, unless you like working 16 hour days, 5-7 days per week, which is what Ryan and Courtney did. Keep in mind these are two separate people – they did not do this together – they each own 400+ niche based Google AdSense websites.

This is by far one of easiest ways to make money but one of the hardest ways to scale successfully, unless you have a proven formula that allows your sites to get ranked on the search engines, almost religiously.

Like the formulas we went over for the process of search engine optimization—hint, hint, wink, wink—when selling space on your websites for advertising, you have a few different options. For one, you can sign up with an ad network like Google AdSense or info links and place a snippet of code on your website and let the ad serving network take care of the rest.

When you do this, advertisers that are writing ads on the advertiser side of the network are choosing where they would prefer to have their ads placed. The publisher or webmaster side of the spectrum just installs the Code and tracks the effectiveness of the ads on the network (effectiveness meaning revenue potential).

In this case you are a publisher. You are a publisher if you are selling ad placement space on YOUR website. Your are an advertiser if you are buying ad placements or space on publisher's websites.

Here is an A – Z list of ad-serving networks you can sign up with and test to see which network's ads consistently make you the most money:

http://onlinebusiness.about.com/od/affiliatemarketing/tp/online-advertising-networks.htm

Ad networks are great as a means to a fast solution to split test different types of ad serving platforms, and obviously, advertisers that write more engaging ads will make you more money because they get clicked on more often.

Bear in mind that some ad networks have different bidding plateaus. Google AdSense has developed a reputation for being one of the stronger ad networks because advertisers are willing to pay more, and let's face it—Google organizes all internet information and serves it to us, so they control the internet. They have authority; they control the web traffic, so they can charge more. They do have high quality traffic because their algorithms are superior and they provide great results based on search queries. Since their engine mystically and magically finds relevant and interested (quality) traffic, they can mark up ad prices like OPEC can flirt with oil prices.

Google's model is not driven by scarcity but by competition (even though I would argue OPEC artificially designs the scarcity associated with their oil so they can pretend supply is low to charge a higher rate than necessary). When you control something that is abundantly useful, you become a king and the only other regulator is government, but anyway enough of politics...

Instead of having your ads brokered through a network to reach advertisers you can cut the cord and reach out to advertisers and offer them your website space. If you are a webmaster looking to sell space on your site, it is easy to find potential buyers. If your site is based on finance, as most of mine are because I love the business and finance niche, simply do a keyword search query in the search engines that could be considered a high quality or high interest keyword.

For my credit repair niche sites, I consider the keyword "credit repair" a high quality keyword, a notion that is based on my results and statistical evidence.

So after you Google the keyword, you will see the ad listings. Make a list of all of the domain names within the sponsored ads. You can now go to http://whois.com to find the email addresses associated with the people who own each of the websites that are advertising on Google. Shoot them a friendly email, telling them that you have traffic that you know would be useful to them.

You can shoot them an offer or a quote—however, whenever you do business, if possible you will want to explain to them all of the key benefits of buying space on your page(s) instead of slapping a price sticker in the email.

After you list all of the benefits they may be willing to pay a higher premium than the number you would settle for, so always let them make an offer first.

Then you can negotiate and kick it up a nickel in order to get maximum dollar out of your pixels.

***

Connecting the dots

- *Buying a domain for 8-10 years is a good idea when considering the authority site model.*
- *Make sure you have a long-term link building strategy in place, with diversification of links and variation of keywords.*
- *Determine how you want to hire people—with a revenue sharing model or a standard payment procedure.*
- *If you choose to hire your team based on a revenue sharing basis, you must act as a strong leader and visionary.*
- *Proper research and strong deductions to connect the keywords to your pages will create a ton of grip and you will be able to get your wheels turning for your authority site.*
- *Affiliate marketing is a great way to make okay money. Know the risks and lack of controls—decide from there.*
- *Sell your own stuff. Hire a team to help you get your product packaged and produced. Inspire an army of affiliates to sell your products that get paid a commission for each sale.*
- *Installing the magical code snippet for ad serving platforms can help you start seeing money right away if you're properly executing the SEO formula.*

Chapter 15: Task Scheduling and Calendar Planning

"Decide upon your major definite purpose in life and then organize all your activities around it."
~Brian Tracy

Without organizing your activities, you will lack the ability to do tasks in the most productive/logical order. Why waste time fumbling about with your project tasks, when you can have a nice clear list to follow and execute?

Making a calendar of events allows you to be more productive, more focused, more efficient and it leads to the creation of tangible results. Making a to-do list, a calendar list, a checklist, or any type of list is something most people don't do, as practical as this well know piece of information is!

It is outlandishly easy to get sidetracked, especially on the internet, with all of the distractions fighting to seize your eyeballs' attention—your email, Facebook, YouTube, etc.

Writing down materials on physical index cards has always helped me. Writing a to-do list and ignoring everything else except the list will help you increase your effectiveness. Making a calendar list is equivalent to making a day-to-day list on steroids. If you can abide by the goals you have listed on each day of the calendar for your new business, then you are taking a step every single day in the right direction. Those steps will add up.

Formulating discipline is among the hardest of all perils a human can tackle. I find it basically impossible to get out of bed in the morning unless a few key things take place. I know myself well enough to forecast whether or not I will be able to escape the warm, comfortable, forever-inviting mattress of mine.

I recently bought a stereo that plays music at 8:00 a.m. every single day, and by the time the 3rd song plays through, I'm able to get out of bed practically dancing.

Oversleeping makes me unhappy and completely ruins the beginning of my day. I'm a time freak, and if my time gets wasted by my own fault or the fault of another, everyone will know it.

I try to sleep only 4-5 hours a day, on purpose, because when we are born we are given a clock that ticks every day towards our demise, I'm not willing to sleep more than needed.

Poly-Phasic sleep patterns appeal to me—sleeping 90-120 minutes a day would be interesting (sleeping 15 minutes at a time, 6 times per day, once every 3-4 hours).

That type of commitment is insane though.

***

Connecting the dots

- *Write down your daily tasks on an index card or sheet of paper.*
- *Making a simple list will make you more productive if you concentrate only on your to-do list.*
- *Save time and get more done with calendar planning!*

Chapter 16: Tracking Progress

"It is the process that is so much stress. It is the progress that feels the best."

~Wayne Carter (Lil Wayne)

If we do not track our efforts, the energy we invest in those efforts will start to crumble. When you build a pyramid (or if you were to), you are able to see it taking shape before your very eyes, and you can measure the progress which propels you to keep hustling till you reach the finish line.

When you build search-based businesses, you will need to track you efforts. You need to know whether or not your money and time is creating numbers that you can measure, and deduce information from in order to keep making informed decisions regarding the direction you must take with your businesses.

Here is a popular SEO (search engine optimization) link tracking tool: http://link-assistant.com/rank-tracker/.

This tool keeps track of your website's SEO rank with the search engines, and when you are executing the link building process; you need to make sure your services are doing their job. Transparency gives us more insight.

Here is a popular tool that measures the hits your website(s) receive: http://statcounter.com.

When you are tracking your website's traffic performance, be sure to un-include your IP address and your employees' IP addresses from your website hit counting stats. There is no need to unintentionally create numbers that are false. False hope is worse than no hope.

***

Connecting the dots

- *Keep track of your link building efforts using the link assistant tool.*
- *Transparency gives us insight and the ability to move forward.*

Chapter 17: The Power of Branded Keywords

"Creativity, as has been said, consists largely of rearranging what we know in order to find out what we do not know. Hence, to think creatively, we must be able to look afresh at what we normally take for granted."
~ George Kneller

Let's change the way we look at keywords, so we can see a new, potent outlet of opportunity. There are two ways to look at keywords: keywords that are based on brands and keywords that are not.

For example, the affiliate website I showed you in (Chapter 11: Real Life Examples of Successful Websites) was not based on the highly competitive keyword "make money online". It was based on a separate branded keyword that echoed this implication.

The six figure program brand stands for "making money online" but it does not have the same characteristics as the original keyword. The competition is much lower and therefore I was able to get ranked easily and make over $6,000 profit in the course of 4 months with just that particular keyword.

Brands create large exposure and awareness in their market. In this case, the six figure program happened to be in the "make money online" type of market.

People buy Hunts or Heinz when they go to the grocery store looking for ketchup –but they don't look for a red bottle that says ketchup on it. They look for their ideal brand.

"Excuse me, may I have a Kleenex?" "No but you can have a tissue."

This example shows the power of a brand's influence on us.

It is past the scope of this book to intimately discuss how to create brands. If you want to learn more about brands, this is your guy: http://draytonbird.com. He knows more about branding and marketing than any normal professional should probably know. I love education and knowledge and I believe everyone should indulge in it. So I don't say that in a bad way—but I think Drayton needs to pick up some new hobbies!

Why are branded keywords so powerful? You can piggyback off of the brand in order to create affiliate-based businesses out of thin air. This is because all of the exposure and advertising has been taken care of.

If you create a website that refers customers to a brand and your website is a spinoff of that brand, then you can hook some of the prospects.

Do not omit the idea of providing some sort of value or insight on your site, so that the entire purpose of the site is not to act as a gateway to or piggyback off of the brand. It should be in your best interest to serve content that is useful or meaningful with the ads or referral links sprinkled around that valued content. This is a safety net so that brands you are marketing for do not get the wrong idea.

Remember, we are working with the merchants as partners. We are not attempting to steal their business, just stimulate it. Product or service reviews work great. Take a product or service that a brand offers and do a positive customer testimonial for the service and slap your affiliate links around your story, then use the SEO formula to shoot traffic at it.

We are now taking on the role of turning potential buyers into actual buyers by erasing their doubts about the service by providing a positive review.

Why is it powerful to use brands as a method of creating profitable businesses? It is much easier to get traffic. Branded keywords by nature are high in volume and low in competition, the two perfect pieces of criteria needed to create profitability.

Here is the correct way to market with branded keywords:

Creating a website such as FlippaReview.com to suggest the pros and cons of the Flippa's buy/sell website services while attaching a referral URL, is a good idea.

Creating a website called BestBuyConsumerProductReviews.com to discuss the good, bad and ugly about products while monetizing the site, is a good idea.

Here is the incorrect way to market with branded keywords:

I actually got threatened by Victoria's Secret Management Stores Inc. and almost had a claim on my hands for registering the domain name VictoriasSecretRewards.com and using it for marketing purposes to make money.

Here is what I didn't think about beforehand:

1) The domain name by nature of how I worded implies that I am in fact Victoria's Secret.
2) The content I placed on the domain further implied that the site was owned and operated by Victoria's Secret.
3) The purpose of the website was to create a profit, not value. I was "i-framing" an affiliate offer. So my affiliate URL which sent traffic to a Victoria's Secret affiliate offer page was my web page.
4) The offer page had fine print which was not attractive if read out loud. I did not own the offer or personally recommend it, but I did market it to others interested in the offer.

Did the site make money? You better believe it.

Was it a bad idea? Yes. The end result: I gave up domain ownership to Victoria's Secret Management Inc.

Do not pretend you are the brand, intentionally or unintentionally. Most big name brands are legally trademarked and they can press charges on you for potentially damaging their brand reputation by pretending to be them and misrepresenting them.

Do not register the domain name bestbuystoresinc.com and pretend to be Best Buy. That is equivalent to stealing their brand identity for the obvious sole purpose of commercial gain.

If you do register a web domain that implies you are the brand (I do this when the brand is not legally trademarked only), make sure you disclose that you are not the brand you appear to be impersonating and that you do not own rights to the brand (even though there are no legal rights) nor are you affiliated (unless you are marketing for the brand) with the brand. Define the purpose of the website and your intent in creating the website in a concise 2 to 3 sentences at the bottom of your web page.

Obviously, you want to cram the value and benefits into this line—as to why your site exists and how it is contributing value to other people's lives.

You do have more wiggle room when a brand is not trademarked. Trademarked brands have access to legal rights to sue you. Brands that *do not* have the trademark® indicated by the "R" do not have full legal rights to the brand. Normally, brands with trademark™ indicated by a "TM" are not legally registered with the United States Patent and Trademark Office: http://www.uspto.gov/.

It is worth it to read through trademark regulations and laws. I once considered registering a trademark and I may file a trademark application in the future, so I educated myself about the trade marking process. It is worth it. I recommend you educate yourself as it is an interesting topic.

So your safest bet with creating branded online businesses is to construct a website around a brand which offers insight into that brand along with some sort of additional value (such as a review that may not be available on the branded website).

The six figure program affiliate-based brand website met this criteria and it continues to excel. A solid piece of my online business revenues are created around this very tactic of using brands to leverage and attract an "almost customers" type of audience.

You can spell out the fact that you are simply a review website easily by implying you are a review website and not the brand itself when you register your domain name. For example, a website entitled: brandreview.com (substitute brand).

The nature of the web address insinuates the purpose of the website. Think in these terms when building businesses around trademarked brands. Just know that doing so is still a risk and if a reputable authority of the brand asks you to take the page down, it is a good idea to comply.

I have not had any problems aside from Victoria's Secret, which was wrong on my part.

***

Connecting the dots

- *Brand-based keywords by nature are low in competition and high in volume.*
- *Creating profitable businesses around branded keywords is an excellent strategy.*
- *Do not imply you are the brand by the wording of your domain name or function of the site itself. If the brand is less known and is not legally trademarked, use your judgment and digression.*
- *In the footer of your website, in a clear and concise manner, define the purpose of your website so that it is obvious you are trying to contribute value to your website visitors.*

Chapter 18: Time Expectancy

"Rome was not built in one day"
~John Heywood

Rome was not built in one day and neither will your business be built in one day. A functioning, profit-yielding online business will not be established in a day or a week, but within a month you can start to build some momentum.

Perhaps the hardest part of creating a successful business is committing to it. Your efforts will seem extreme because you are working for yourself. When you spend time trying to create businesses and you spend money, you are going to naturally expect to make money right away.

This is a common misconception that filters out the business owners who are not willing to be committed to seeing their businesses through till they create profit producing outcomes. A rather embarrassing figure, let's say 97% of people new to business, are impatient and decide to quit when they are a few days or weeks into the venture.

Some may feel like their efforts were in vain or that they were not properly rewarded for their energy and time spent. Working for someone else automatically creates a paycheck and a reward for your efforts. When you work for yourself, your work input determines your paycheck's output, so I'm saying you write your own checks.

If you spend about 3 hours a day working on your business startup, then you can expect to have results that only 3 hours of time and energy spent would produce. If you were to work 8 hours for someone else—would you be willing to work 16 or 20 hours a day for yourself when you are not limited by work shift barriers?

I certainly used this to my advantage when I started. Freedom comes at a price and that is relentless willingness to work like crazy in the beginning so you can have free time later. Would you rather work 40 years for someone else so that you save enough money to retire and be financially self-sufficient in your remaining 10-15 years on this planet? Or would you rather spend 2 years creating a wealth system that will keep you wealthier and happier than most for the next 50-60 years of your existence?

I don't know about you, but I will work hard upfront and sit back and relax later. Time is limited, money is not. Approximately $1 trillion dollars in transactions through international commerce take place every single day. Everyone breathing on this planet has a number or destination they reach and they expire. It is simply how our current life cycle works.

Your financial number, your wealth—you can control. You can control how you spend your time. You cannot control your age, and you are getting older every second, just like me. But it's never too late to change your financial number. If you have 5 years left in the workforce until your retirement you can still choose to work hard for 2 years to get 3 extra years out of your retirement, and who knows—if you play your cards right, you will have more wealth and ultimately more freedom and ultimately more happiness.

So what can I say about how long this should take? It will be based on your work input. The amount of work you put into your business will determine the results or successes by which you can measure your work output.

Why do I make well into the 5 figure mark each month and why do I have days where I clear $6,000 in profit? I have been creating profitable businesses out of thin air for a few months now, but I have only been in the "business world" for about 1 year and some change. But, I worked those 12 hour days on my businesses 7 days a week while *working two jobs* and going to a prestigious *tech school* for Computer Forensics at the same time (you can check out the college I used to attend here: http://rit.edu).

The above example proves you can do it. I hear the argument every day from people who feel otherwise. One of my best friends tells me frequently, "Justin, not everyone can work the way you do, not everyone is built to work hours on end to chase something that seems endless."

Julie is hands down one of the smartest people I know and I agree with her on this issue. Business ownership is not for everyone. Nationwide statistics prove it. 9% of our American population own businesses, not taking into account children. 1% of our American population is in control of 99% of the wealth.

You can be a part of the one percent too, just know what to expect, and triumph.

***

Connecting the dots

- *Creating a profitable business is an event caused by an energy fueled process.*
- *Time, focus and energy are the ingredients of productivity.*
- *Productivity leads to progress which leads to successful business creation.*
- *Master the art of being productive and you take sizeable steps each and every day to being well on your way to a financially free life.*

Part 3: On Pay Per Click (PPC) Advertising

Chapter 19: What is Pay Per Click?

"If we did all the things we were capable of doing, we would literally astound ourselves."
~Thomas Edison

I believe that with a little bit of know-how, anyone can be capable of setting up a pay per click advertising campaign and start making money on the internet.

Pay per click is paid, targeted, search advertising. You pay only when a person clicks on your advertisement. You also can choose to show ads to people who are already very likely interested in your offer, product or service only. When harnessed properly Pay per click advertising will create a whole new scale of internet customers for your business, almost instantly.

Setting up a pay per click marketing campaign consists mainly of two components: your ads and your keywords. You bid on the keywords that you would like your ads to appear for. When the keywords trigger your ads, your ad competes with other ads that are bidding on the keyword. If your ad is more compelling than your competition's, you gain the click-thru and the possibility of turning that prospect into a customer by means of your website.

When Google's pay per click platform known as Adwords was created, a few entrepreneurs who realized the incredible opportunity to gain customers virtually became millionaires overnight. The entrepreneurs who had been keeping an eye on the power of the search engines to connect with customers suddenly had a way to get on the first page of Google's search results without having to play by the SEO rules.

Although nowadays the competition in Google Adwords is huge, there are still plenty of opportunities to make a profit by using their Adwords platform for advertising.

Pay per click is often used by solo marketers also known as "affiliates" because unlike SEO, you do not have to wait 4-8 weeks to start seeing traffic come into your websites. Whether the traffic is profitable or not will be based on how well you can read your data in order to make necessary changes.

The general rule of thumb with pay per click advertising is to spend less than you earn from sales revenue. In order to transform your pay per click campaigns from a negative return on investment to a positive one, you will have to make sure you have a competent tracking system in place. More on this in (Chapter 23: On Tracking).

Unfortunately, when advertising in any media channel, what should *logically* do well may do worse and what should have logically done okay or moderate can prove to be the best venue for ad space.

What does this mean in relation to pay per click advertising campaigns? The keywords that your ads are showing up with may be a great fit for your campaign or they may simply not create the end result you are looking for. All the more reason to track your statistics to see what is actually working.

***

Connecting the dots

- *Pay per click is paid, targeted search advertising.*
- *Pay per click campaigns consist of ads that are triggered by keywords you place bids on.*

- *The pay per click market is competitive, but with a little bit of energy and a competent tracking system in place, the opportunities are huge.*

Chapter 20: On Campaigns

"The majority see the obstacles; the few see the objectives; history records the successes of the latter, while oblivion is the reward of the former."
~ Alfred Armand Montapert

Knowing everything you can about what you are doing is a great way to arm yourself with the ability to destroy obstacles and focus on objectives. Many try to make pay per click work, but in reality they do not understand much about what it is they are doing.

So the objective gets buried under the small obstacles that can be easily bypassed with a little bit of knowledge. Be part of the latter, not the former. The intention of this chapter is to explain in a transparent fashion what a pay per click campaign is all about and how to set one up without confusion.

First, what is a "campaign" in regards to marketing?

Wikipedia defines the "action" of being involved in a campaign as follows: *"To work in an organized and active way toward a particular goal, typically a political or social one."*

In our case, our goal is to create a PPC campaign that consists of a winning combination of ads + keywords + landing pages, in order to sell something of value while generating a profit.

Components of a pay per click campaign:

1. Campaign settings
2. Ad group settings
3. Ad text
4. Keywords

We'll go through these one by one in detail.

1. Campaign settings

Campaign settings govern the entire campaign, meaning these settings will override any ad group settings. You have the ability to make specific changes that apply only to certain ad groups.

An ad group contains two things, a categorized list of keywords and two corresponding ads. One ad at a time will be triggered to display when a keyword your are bidding on has been searched, rotating with the other ad based on your settings.

When you set up a campaign these are the settings you will have to configure. I will take you through each type of setting, step-by-step. Note: these steps apply to Google Adwords and Microsoft Adcenter.

A) Languages and locations

Do the people you are selling to speak English only? If you are writing your ads and landing pages in the English language, then only allow your ads to appear to people who speak English for this campaign. If you are promoting an affiliate offer and the offer owner does not want customers outside the U.S., do not bother serving your ads outside the U.S.

So are you selling to the United States or Singapore?

Yes you can have your ads served internationally. Just select which country to show your ads. You can get even more specific and serve your ads to specific regions within a country as well. For example, you can choose to have your ads serve in New York, within just one major city in New York. So you be geographically specific if you prefer.

B) Networks and devices

Devices

You can choose to specify which places you would like your ads to appear and also which types of devices it will appear on (phones, laptops, desktops, and tablets). The type of devices you want to show your ads on will vary with your offer. If you are marketing a mobile phone offer it makes sense to show your ads on mobile devices. If you are selling something that requires the person to read a long page or watch a video, it does not make sense for you to show your ads to mobile users. They will likely click on your ad and leave because it does not load fast enough, which is a waste of your money and their time.

Even more important than devices are networks. In Google Adwords and Microsoft Adcenter, you can choose where you want your ads to be distributed. 99% of marketers set up this part of their campaigns wrong.

You do not want to mix a combination of different ad distribution sources together within the same campaign. Mixing your networks and/or distribution settings into one single campaign will create an excellent variety of confusion and less reliable tracking.

Why?

Google Adwords and Microsoft Adcenter have three separate places that you can serve your ads and each place is 100% different then the other.

You could have a negative campaign that could become profitable by simply disabling a particular ad network/distribution setting that is sucking away all of your money and likewise, you can make more money by expanding your ad reach.

What is the solution?

You divide each campaign that contains your ad groups (which consist of your keywords and ads) into 3 separate campaigns. Each campaign will contain the same ads, keywords and landing pages. The difference between each of the 3 campaigns that have the same keywords and ads will be the place in which the ads are served.

Networks

These are three separate ad networks/distributions:

1. Search
2. Search Partners
3. Content Network, also known as the Display Network

1) Search (Highest Quality Traffic Available and Most Expensive)

Search traffic means you are showing your ads on Google's search engine only (Google Adwords) or likewise, you are showing your ads on Yahoo and Bing's search engines only (Microsoft Adcenter).

As we discussed earlier, search traffic is the nirvana of quality traffic for advertising because the web searcher is already interested in what you are offering and this makes your job as an internet salesmen much easier. Persuading someone to buy your product or sign up for your service who is not previously interested in your product or service is much more difficult.

With search, you can rightfully assume that the person has a genuine interest in whatever it is you are offering and if the benefits promised to them outweigh the costs, then they will take you up on your offer.

Showing up unannounced to someone's doorstep to sell pots and pans will be hard because your prospect may not be interested in pots and pans at all. If they have no intention on buying, even if they listen to your incredible sales pitch, they will still not buy simply because they never got interested, even after you cram the benefits into their ears.

Search traffic provides you will people who are interested in what you have to offer. This makes the ability to profit using SEO and PPC as a means to finding customers incredibly popular. This is why more money is spent on search engine based ad platforms for internet advertising than any other form of internet ads and this is also why it is the most competitive. Some companies are willing to pay $20.00 for a single click, or more.

Could you imagine that?

They obviously have a powerful sales process to make up for their heavy upfront investments and/or a heavy duty ad budget. More on sales process in (Chapter 36: On Sales Process).

2) Search Partners (Less Interested Search-Based Traffic)

Search partner traffic means:

- Your ads are being listed or displayed when a web surfer is on a website that has a “search plug-in” which is a miniaturized search bar for which they can search content.
- The search bar will be sponsored, which means it will return ad listings based on the keywords you are bidding on

Non-sponsored search bars will return content and/or page listings on the site itself based on the keywords search. Those are not search partner ad listings.

This traffic source can be a huge asset as long as you track effectively and eliminate bad traffic sources. More on this in (Chapter 23: On Tracking).

Search partner traffic is simply lower quality search-based traffic often from little websites that can be in the same niche of what you are advertising, or they can be completely outside your niche. The further away the search partners are from your niche, the less valuable the traffic will likely be. If someone does a sponsored search on a cooking website for “credit repair” then the person doing the search will not likely be as valuable as if they were to skip the cooking site and do a direct search for “credit repair” on Google/Yahoo or Bing.

The average cost per click for search partner ads is lower because the quality of the clicks is lower.

But I have some great days with a 2600% return on investment from Microsoft Adcenter’s search partner network. To put that into perspective, I spent roughly $1 on a few clicks that led to $260.00 in sales revenue. So yes, sometimes you can really hit a home run with the search partner network despite the quality of your clicks being less.

Other times, I have used the search partner network and spent $80-$100 to barely make back the cost of the traffic. You have a lot of factors in your control to shift your campaigns from red to green, which we will be discussing momentarily.

The golden rule of thumb with search partner traffic is to exclude search partner websites sending you high volumes of traffic with low returns. Once you refine the campaign, your return on investment will start to fly into the clouds.

3) Content Network also Known as the Display Network

Content traffic means:

- You are showing your ad on a website such as a blog. This is called a placement.
- You can write a text ad or use an image to be displayed on your placements.
- You can indicate which websites you want your ads to be placed on. Google Adwords allows you to specify your ad placements down to each individual website.

In order for your ad placement to show up on the indicated website, that website must be a part of the Google AdSense (Google) or info links (Yahoo/Bing).

With Microsoft Adcenter you can choose to place your ads on the "Microsoft Network" you then have the ability to generate reports in Adcenter to see which individual websites in the network sent you traffic and if any placements were negative or profitable. You can then exclude the websites in the network that did not do well. So with Adcenter you have limited control over your ad placements in their content network.

Let's look at an example of someone going through a process that leads him/her to clicking on an ad placement that is on a website.

Suppose this person in our example is curious about learning how to discipline him/herself in order to become more productive, efficient and confident. The person goes to Google.com and types in the search: *how to discipline yourself*

The person stumbles upon a great blog that has information about increasing your productivity, efficiency and confidence by disciplining yourself. When the person is done reading the blog page he/she feels good because he/she learned something new regarding a topic he/she was curious about.

After he/she finished reading the page, he/she notices a blue underlined text link that says:

Become More Productive!
Learn How to Become More Productive, Efficient and Confident.
Millions of Copies Sold. Get Access Today For Only $1.
www.ProductivityKit.com

This ad is extremely relevant to what the person is interested in. The chances that this person clicks on this ad are very high. The chances that the advertiser who placed their ad on the blog are going to get a new customer are also high. The blog-owner (publisher) will make a small profit for delivering an ad click-thru and the advertiser (producer) will potentially get a new customer to buy their products or services. It's a win/win situation.

The advertiser who is selling their productivity kit just got an extremely qualified click-thru from the ad placement that most likely costs a fraction of a search based click.

When you enable the content network on Google Adwords you have two options. You can use Google's Ad Planner to do research on places to put your ad and you can make a list of the websites you want your ad(s) to be placed on.

The second option is to let Google decide where to place your ads. When you go this route, you can get a large amount of impressions (views) in your display account so you can measure your ad's click through rates (CTR). Google's ad placing program will keep track of which websites your ads were served on. It will also make a note of the clicks your ads got and on which websites led to the clicks. The program will then serve your add less on websites that did not get ad clicks, and more on sites that did get ad clicks.

Your other option is to do competitive research using tools such as:

- Mixrank – http://mixrank.com
- WhatRunsWhere – http://whatrunswhere.com

These tools can show you stuff like where your competitors are placing their ads, the ad copy they are using, how many clicks their ad(s) have received since the ad was placed, and how long the ad has been in the designated placement.

You should be aware of who your competitors are. You should keep an eye on what they are doing so you can stay ahead of the curve. You are the one who should aspire to be the trendsetter—make them copy you. You can also gain some useful insight by looking at their ad data.

If an advertiser has had an ad placement listed on websiteXYZ for 2 years and the ad listed on websiteXYZ has received 80,000 clicks over the course of two years, then this likely means it is a profitable ad placement.

Since your product or service is in the same niche as your competitor, chances are you could gain an income producing ad placement on the same website. You can learn from their data that they spent tons of money and time on acquiring.

So what should you expect when you enable the content network?

At first you will likely get lots of impressions and very few clicks. You can choose to shuffle banner ads into your ad placements. Banner ads will have a much better chance of getting clicked on than a text ad. Let's face it: Images are more exciting than words.

Refining your ads to become more appealing is a never-ending process, especially on this network of advertising because there are so many impressions and opportunities to get customers.

Tracking your ads will involve keeping a close eye on the metrics inside your Adwords account. After you are able to convert some impressions into clicks, the next step is to filter out the good quality traffic referral sources from the not so good ones.

C) Bidding Options and Your Budget

I always manually set my bids instead of letting Google decide what my bids should be. Each keyword that you would like to have your ad served for can have a separate MCPC, which is the maximum cost per click you are willing to spend on that keyword. For one keyword I may only want to bid $2.50 and for another maybe I only would like to bid $1.00, so I make the adjustments accordingly.

Make sure to configure your campaign to allow you to choose your bids. The alternative is to have Google decide what your maximum bid should be, based on what your competitors are paying. You do not want to set up your bids this way.

When you first start advertising on a new ad platform, keep your budget under or around $100 per day (or whatever you are comfortable with potentially losing). Advertising dollars buy data and data determines profitability. So always set your daily budget to a figure that you are comfortable with when you are first starting out. There are people who have lost thousands of dollars within a few hours of letting their ads run because they did not properly indicate a maximum spending budget.

D) Day Parting and Time Scheduling

Google Adwords and Microsoft Adcenter allow you to pick which time of the day and day of the week you would like your ads to be served.

Google allows you to determine your ad scheduling times right down to 15 minute time intervals. This gives you more control over your campaign. If your data consistently points out the fact that during a certain part of the day or day of the week, you lose money, then you can disable your ads for that day or time period within that day to create a better profit margin.

Microsoft is not as flexible as Google when it comes to ad serving times. Adcenter allows you to indicate times in block form only:

1. 3 AM – 7 AM (early morning)
2. 7AM – 11 AM (morning)
3. 11AM – 2PM (midday)
4. 2PM – 6PM (afternoon)
5. 6PM – 11PM (evening)
6. 11PM – 3AM(late night)

Plainly put, you have less control on Adcenter for ad serving times than on Adwords.

E) Ad Delivery (Rotation)

Google Adwords has an ad delivery, which means ad “rotation” setting. It allows you to have more control over how your ads are shown.

You can choose to have Google show an ad that has the best click-thru rate for the day or you can choose to show both ads evenly. Or you can choose to have Google automatically show the ad that generates the most conversions out of the two within your ad group.

I always set this setting to rotate ads evenly. When both of your ads are shown evenly, you can make your own assessment as to which ad is more effective in generating clicks and then you can rewrite the loser ad to try and make it better than the winning ad.

Microsoft Adcenter does not have an ad delivery feature.

2. Ad Group Settings

With Adcenter, you can choose to have specific settings for each ad group, so in this case you have more control over your individual ad group settings on Adcenter than on Adwords.

The most relevant ad group setting you would be most likely to change, if any, would be the networks/ad distribution settings. You would not need to do this if you break your campaign into 3 campaigns to track each of the network distribution results.

These ad group settings can be useful if you plan on mixing your network settings together. Other than that, there is not any particular use for these additional settings.

3. Ad Text

How do you write a good ad?

When you are writing ads, the key is to focus on differentiating your ad from your competitors'. We want to prove to the web searcher that our service is superior to our competitor's product or service, and we can do this by writing a more compelling ad.

Outlining the benefits of clicking on your ad is not always enough. You don't have to write perfect ads for each ad group the first time you set up your campaign. You will have plenty of chances to refine your ad to make it the best it can be.

Whenever you get ready to write an ad think about the following:

- How can I word my ad so that is sounds like I'm providing more value than my competitors' ads?
- How can I say/provide better benefits (with better proof of the benefits) in my ad than my competitors' ads?

Studying your competitors' ads will allow you to see what you are up against so you have a basis for what direction to take.

Do not get discouraged when reading your competitors ads. They are counting on you to think they have the market on lockdown so you will be discouraged and less likely to compete with them.

Whenever I look at my competitor's ads, I laugh because I can think of multiple ways to write better ads then the ones they are currently running. Some people think they understand how to advertise in their market, and some do, but more often, they do not. I actually get more encouraged to enter certain markets when I see how weak and pathetic my competition is.

I have learned that including statistical proof by putting numbers in your ads works great. Benefits and proof of your benefits with actual numbers will create powerful ads.

Take a look at the ads shown next. These ads are the results returned from the Google search keyword: weight loss.

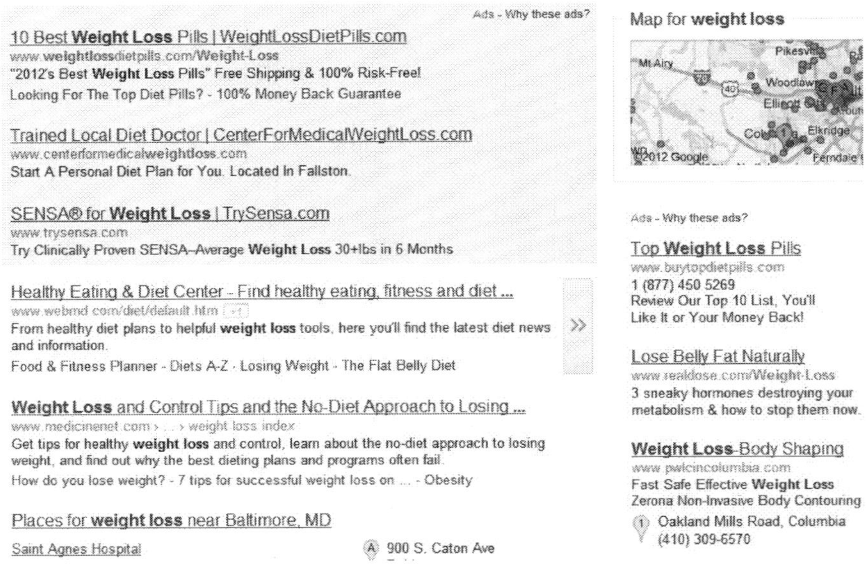

The ad in the #1 spot is WeightLossDietPills.com. Here is what they are doing right:

1. They are describing their benefits—with proof—inside the ad body.
2. They put quotations around their proof element for a more personalized touch.
3. They focused on solving major inconveniences of weight loss pills by explaining there is free shipping and the offer is 100% risk free, meaning there must be some sort of guarantee in case the customer is not satisfied with the product.

Here is what they did wrong:

1. In the second line of the body part in their ad, they waste valuable ad space by saying: "Looking for the top diet pills? 100% money back guarantee." The person reading the ad should already understand that "100% risk free" implies that there is a guarantee in place that will be further explained on the landing page. There is no need to repeat the same benefit twice.

2. The person who wrote the ad should have jam-packed more elements of proof or more benefits in their second line of the body text.

   Here is an example for a better line 2: *Lose 15lbs in 30 days, increase your metabolism and energy—Guaranteed.*

   That statement is way better. It adds three additional benefits of clicking on that ad, and the "guaranteed" part is the icing on the cake. It just sounds so matter of fact. It's hard to argue with the claims in that sentence.

   Obviously, I would predict my ad would win against the current person who has the #1 position.

Take a second and go through the other ads and run the ad copy through your filters, thinking about the following as you read:

- What benefits are the ads claiming?
- Is there proof in the ad?
- Is there numerical proof? (i.e. 15 lbs in 30 days)
- Is the ad relevant to the keyword?

The saying "numbers don't lie" is popular for a reason. Numbers work better than alphabetic characters ever will with ads—keep that in mind when framing your ad copy.

4. Keywords:

Step 1: Use a keyword tool to get a list of ideas/suggestions.

I personally use: https://adwords.google.com/select/KeywordToolExternal

The purpose of this tool is to enter a keyword such as "weight loss" to gain a list of approximately 800 or more related search queries that are Googled on a monthly basis.

Sign up for your Google Adwords account and you will be able to use this tool without having to enter a captcha every time you do a search. A captcha is a pass-code you will be prompted to enter in order to continue what you are doing—it is basically a pop up verifying that you are a human.

Step 2: Theme the keywords, meaning organize them based on their similarities, into separate groups. This will allow you to write ads that are specific and related to all of the keywords in that group. You can have a list of 10 keywords that are closely related to each other in one ad group—each of the keywords will trigger one of the two ads you wrote for that designated keyword. I use the keyword grouper tool. It is not free (I believe it is around $29), but it is well worth it.

It will take a list of 2 - 10,000+ keywords and categorize them into groups for you to make your job easier.

Step 3: The next logical step is to start creating your ad groups inside your Adwords or Adcenter account—however you do not want to do this for Adwords. You will see why in the following chapter.

After you have your keyword groups categorized into separate ad groups, you can write two ads for each ad group. You can do this offline—be sure to make use of the adcenter desktop tool and the Adwords desktop tool. These tools allow you to setup campaigns on your computer as opposed to doing it online, using the Adwords/Adcenter interfaces.

The desktop tools also have features available that the online interface does not. One particular feature I like is the ability to quickly duplicate campaigns to change the ad distributions. For instance: taking one campaign, making two copies, then specifying search partners only for one, content network only for one, and plain search for the last.

Step 4: Anytime you upload a campaign from your desktop publisher tools or manually set up a campaign online, you want to make sure your LP (landing page) is already set up correctly.

Google, Yahoo and Bing have "quality scores" which label your site to a numerical grade of 0-10 (much like SEO page rank—only with PPC now). The keyword you are bidding on, the relevancy of the ad and the relevancy of your LP (landing page) will dictate your quality score.

The higher your quality score, the less you pay, the more traffic you get, and the more money you make, period. There are no exceptions. If you want to make money doing PPC, appease the quality score metric or get funneled out of the game.

You have to do the on-page optimization stuff for your LP that is receiving the PPC traffic. Much like SEO, you have to be as relevant as possible. Sometimes this means creating a LP for each and every single keyword, or at a minimum, one LP per ad group.

More on quality scores in the following chapter...

***

Connecting the dots

- *Like anything in life, knowing everything you can about something will help you succeed in it. Make sure you understand pay per click on an intimate level.*
- *Separate each of your campaigns into 3 individual campaigns. Each campaign will have one ad distribution feature enabled: one search, one search partners and one with the content network.*
- *Make sure you understand the campaign settings.*
- *Due diligence pays in PPC as it does with SEO or anything in life. Do research on your competitors; learn as much as you can. Do Your Homework.*
- *Practice identifying weak points in your competitor's ads. Not only will you get better at writing your own ads, but you will develop an eye for easy markets.*

Chapter 21: On Adwords

"Courage is going from failure to failure without losing enthusiasm"
~Winston Churchill

Setting up a successful pay per click campaign requires you to be courageous. It requires determination and enthusiasm. Chances are you will lose money up front, and despite knowing this, you still have to be courageous and risk it.

Even if the majority of your campaigns start off as failures or prove to be a failure, you cannot lose your enthusiasm. You have to remind yourself that persistence creates perseverance. You can succeed in creating profitable businesses with pay per click.

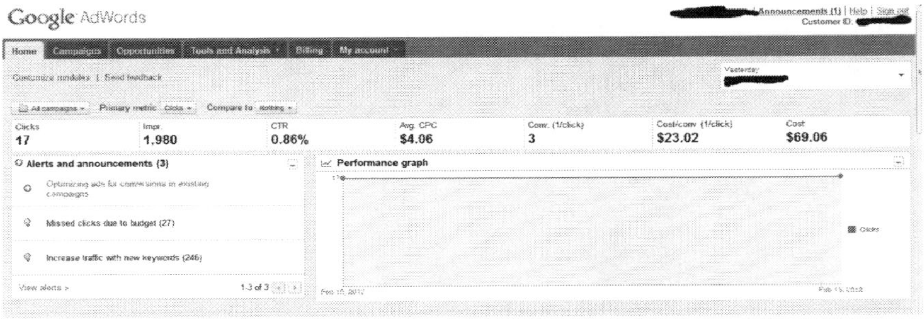

The above screenshot shows one of my Google Adwords campaigns running for part of the day on a week day. This particular campaign usually stems a 33% return on investment. This is equivalent to spending $1 to make $1.33. Now if I spend over $2,000 a month in ad costs, then the left-over revenue for this example would be greater than $3,000.

Let's talk about some of Google's Adwords polices.

Unfortunately, it is hard for affiliate marketers to try and sell stuff using Adwords traffic. Likewise, it is difficult to advertise with them if you do not own the product or service you are selling. So if you are planning to advertise as an affiliate you have to take a few different things into account.

When you are writing your ads, the last part of completing your ad is to specify the domain name you want to send the traffic to. Make sure you do not place an affiliate link inside the destination address of your ads.

This will get your Adwords account a warning. One of Google's policies is that your display URL and destination URL have the same domain name.

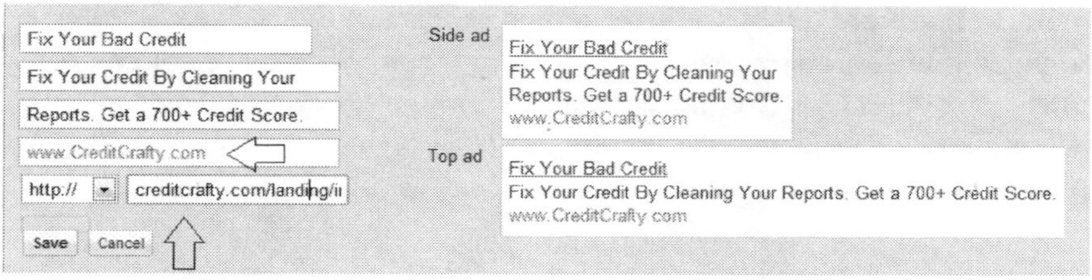

In the picture above you can see that my credit website creditcrafty.com is in the display URL field and in the destination URL field.

Most affiliate links that you use to promote affiliate programs are unique tracking links, so the URL will NOT be the same as the final landing page URL that your affiliate link re-directs to. You do not want to place your affiliate link inside the destination link box.

The way around this, is to create your own landing page (that you own) with the purpose of getting people to click on the affiliate link on your landing page, so they are then re-directed to the offer you are promoting.

But even if you are one of Google's best customers—meaning you spend a ton of money advertising with them—they will not hesitate to ban your account if your violate their polices more than once. Google does not like affiliate landing pages. So the trick is to make your landing page not to appear as an affiliate landing page. Google refers to these types of pages as "gateway" pages, meaning their only purpose is to get someone to go to another page.

Google believes in providing the best search experience possible to users who are clicking on the ads that they are serving. They do not believe a page that has the objective of getting the person to another page is a good search experience.

There is a way around this gateway or bridge page problem. The answer is simpler than you may think: Simply add more pages to your website that aim to provide value to the users clicking on your ads that are landing on your web pages.

Creating one page can be tedious, so creating multiple pages would require an article writer to help supplement the one page website.

Naturally, there are "black hat" methods for avoiding the polices Google has put in place. I do not usually partake in these methods because I'm usually compliant with Google's policies, however, there is a way to "cloak" which means hide your real landing page from Google Adword's ad review team.

You do this by means of sending the person through a "User-Agent" filter and an "ip-address" filter. If either of one of those filters determines that the person clicking on that link is associated with Google, the person will be directed to a "compliant web page" while the others, (non-Google personnel) are directed to the actual page you are using for your campaign.

This idea is difficult to implement unless you have a few tools in your belt, in which case it is not so complex. But, my intent with this book is not to break Adwords polices, it is to teach you how to advertise legitimately and provide value to your customers.

Adwords is thick with competition because there are many big name advertisers with six figure ad budgets that can put up ridiculous bids on keywords that most affiliates or solo marketers cannot compete with. It does not make it impossible to compete, it just makes your margins thinner and the risk greater. The credit card market for example, is a popular market that everyone feels the need to jump into.

Newbie's would do much better if they refrained from this 800 pound gorilla. I made the same mistake—I tried to get a slice of the credit card market, and it did not happen. It did not happen because I stopped trying to compete against fully staffed incorporated companies who could afford to bid over $5.00 a click on an ad. I do compete in the competitive credit repair services niche and I do well in it as an affiliate. I can afford to pay $4.00 per click and remain profitable.

Keyword	Clicks	Cost	CTR	Impr.	Conv. (1/click)	Cost/conv. (1/click)	Conv. rate (1/click)
credit repair	6	$30.82	1.12%	538	1	$30.82	16.67%
clean your credit report	1	$2.75	11.11%	9	0	$0.00	0.00%
fix your credit score	0	$0.00	0.00%	174	0	$0.00	0.00%
fix your credit score	0	$0.00	0.00%	0	0	$0.00	0.00%
fix your credit score	0	$0.00	0.00%	0	0	$0.00	0.00%

View saved filter » 1-5 of 99

The screenshot shown is a preview window of some of the keyword metrics in an Adwords account. Below, I have defined all of the relevant metrics you will need to know. Not all metrics are visible in the screenshot.

Adwords metrics

- **Keyword** – this column indicates which keyword you are bidding on
- **Status** – this column tells you if your keyword is triggering your ads or if it is not
- **Max CPC** – this is a numerical metric that simply means: what is the maximum you are willing to pay for 1 click for this keyword? Meaning, for example, are you willing to pay up to $3.00 for a click for the keyword: "keyword"?

- **Quality score** – this is much like the "page rank" for SEO stuff. Now it is applied towards your pay per click campaign. Your quality score has tremendous weight on how much you have to pay for the keywords you want to advertise with. The higher your quality score, (0 – 10) the less you have to pay to get the same if not better, ad position rankings (the higher the better!)
- **Clicks** – the number of clicks your keyword has received for the dates specified
- **Impressions** – the number of times a person saw or viewed your ad
- **Click through rate** – if 100 people saw your ad and 1 person clicked it, this means you have a 1% click-thru rate. Simply clicks divided by impressions.
  *Ex: 100 clicks / 3,431 impressions = .029 click-thru rate. Round up and move the decimal over two places and your click through rate for this example equals about 3%, which is good. Three people clicked on your ad; 100 saw your ad.
- **Average CPC** – you will be charged different amounts every time a person clicks on your ad for a particular keyword. Google determines what to charge you each time based on certain elements such as your ad's click-thru rate, your quality score, etc. Your average cost is essentially: Cost / # of clicks
  *Ex: $60 divided by 20 clicks = average cost per click of $3.00
- **Cost** – the total amount of money you have spent on that keyword
- **Average Position** – the ad's position (1 - 8) when stacked up against competitors also bidding on that keyword. So it is essentially what ad slot or ad position you are in for that keyword.
- **Conversion per click** – "How many clicks does it take to get a conversion?" is what this metric is asking. So if you have 10 clicks and 1 conversion, on average it takes 10 clicks to get a conversion.
- **Cost per conversion** – "How much does it cost to get a conversion?" is what this metric calculates based on your data. So if you spend $30 on 10 clicks or $3 per click like the above example, then it costs $30.00 to get a conversion. If a conversion is equal to a $45.00 sale then you have a net profit of $15 for every $30 you spend, if the conversion rate is consistent.

- **Conversion rate** – clicks divided by conversions. If you have 100 clicks and 6 conversions, you have a 6% conversion rate, i.e. 6% of your traffic becomes a lead or sale.
- **View through conversion** – is the number of people who come to your website and do not covert into a sale or lead at first, but later on come back and decide to become a conversion. This will be another percentage and is a good metric to look at for "re-marketing", which means to keep trying to sell to someone who was previously interested in your stuff but did not take action.

How to get a better quality score and widen up your profit margin

Quality scores for your keywords on Adwords are crucial to your ability to make Adwords a profitable traffic source. We now know that it can be difficult to make a campaign profitable if we have to spend more than we can possibly make back.

When you have low quality scores for the keywords you want your ads to show for, you have to pay more to get your ad noticed. When I say more, I mean "a lot more". I know from others' experiences as well as my own.

Let me give you an example. One Adwords blunder I made early on was to ignore the quality score principle; I got hit with keyword quality scores of 3's and 4's. The estimated cost to get my ad listed on the first page of Google was $8.50. It is kind of difficult to make a profitable campaign when you're spending almost a $10 dollar bill to get one person to see your website.

Later on I made sure to pay special attention to the quality scores of my keywords and the following time, my keywords had quality scores of 6's, 7's, and 8's. For the same keyword, my estimated ad cost to get on the front page was $3.50.

Unreal? You bet it is! It costs $5 less per click to get the same ad positioning! Imagine if you got a quality score of 10 for some keyword! (Which I have done and I can tell you it is sweet).

I had a quality score of 10 for a few different keywords and I did not have to spend more than a quarter for extremely qualified traffic—that is the secret sauce to making your campaigns explosively profitable.

So how do you make sure to get a solid quality score?

1. You will have to register a new domain name if you already put a domain name into a Google ad that got you a bad quality score in the past. Sorry, but Google doesn't give second chances for domain names.
2. Your landing page is the page your ad is sending the traffic to. Much like doing on-page optimization with SEO, you need to do the same exact thing for the page you are sending your PPC traffic to.
   This means that you will want to mention the keyword you are bidding on, or a close variant of it, more than a few times. The way to be most effective with this is to literally put each keyword in its own ad group and have a landing page that mentions your keyword 4-5 times. Time consuming? It can be, unless you outsource! Booya!
   So if you have 2 ads that are competing with each other for best CTR, and they are triggered from the keyword that has an amazingly relevant landing page, this is a good start.
3. Your ads + keywords - Put your keyword in your ad title (if you can—some keywords are too long). Place your keyword in your ad body, and if it fits, you can place a sub or slug on your display link address for added relevancy.
   Examples:

   Typical domain ad display link: MyAdDisplayLink.com or MyAdDisplayLink.com

   Adding a sub: **MyKeyword**.MyAdDisplayLink.com

   Adding a slug: MyAdDisplayLink.com/**MyKeyword**

   Mix and match to see what gets the best CTR. This is anyone's game and testing is king.

One last piece of advice is to bid a little bit higher than the minimum bid required to get your ad listed on the first page. This will show Google that you are serious. This will also positively affect your quality score because bid is a factor and a higher quality score will save you money in the long run.

Recap to ensure a high quality score for your keyword(s):

1. Mention your keyword in your ad title and ad body and possibly add your keyword as a slug or sub to your display link domain
2. Make sure your landing page mentions your keyword 4 – 5 times. Period.
3. Bid higher than the minimum upfront to show Google you are serious. This will have a positive effect on your quality scores for your keywords.
4. Reap the benefits of much larger profit margins because your quality score is higher than your competitors!

***

Connecting the dots

- *It takes courage to set up a pay per click campaign because you risk losing money. Stay enthusiastic and learn as much as possible from your failures and your successes.*
- *Make a conscious effort to follow Google's Adwords policies so you do not lose your account.*
- *Study and understand the Adwords keyword metrics.*
- *Take extra time to ensure you get good quality scores. You will make a lot more money, no exceptions.*

Chapter 22: On Adcenter

"Success seems to be connected with action. Successful people keep moving. They make mistakes, but they don't quit."
~Conrad Hilton (Hilton Hotels)

If you wish to experience success with pay per click, you need to set up a pay per click campaign many times – now, let's talk about Microsoft Adcenter!

Adcenter is the result of the two search engines Yahoo and Bing combining to form one ad serving platform. Adcenter is a much better place to start with pay per click than Google Adwords for a few different reasons.

The main reason is that it costs less, plain and simple. The costs are half that of Adwords and sometimes even lower.

I have been able to target and bid on keywords that typically cost $3 for entry on Adwords for only $1 on Adcenter. I base this information on a few different pay per click campaigns that have cumulatively made over $30,000 in revenue in the finance niche.

I have noticed that Adwords traffic turned into sales more often than Adcenter traffic. However, the profit margins in Adcenter for the finance campaigns were much greater. It is simply because I paid 66% less for traffic that converts almost as well.

For example, for the same niche and same keywords, I can spend $100 on 42 Adwords clicks, which creates an average cost per click of about $2.38. Normally my average cost per lead (CPL) was around $22-$25 in Adwords which means 1 in 10 clicks would turn into a lead. This means I had a 10% conversion rate.

On average, one out of 3 Adwords leads would convert into a sale. Let's say I get paid on average, about $80 for a sale. So that means it costs me $66-$75 to get a sale with Google Adwords traffic. So I'm making a slim profit according to these metrics.

With Adcenter I can spend around $5-$7 for one lead in the same niche with the same or very similar keywords. So if I have 17 leads for one day from the Adcenter traffic and I only spend $100, my cost per lead is $5.88. With Adcenter, about 1 in 7 leads would turn into a sale, opposed to 1 in 3 leads turning into a sale with Google.

This is how I'm able to deduce that Google traffic is more qualified for my offer. However, do not forget the fact that it now only costs about $41.16 to get an $80.00 sale.

The lesson here is that the "highest quality" traffic will normally come at a price, unless you tap into a high quality traffic source—which you can do with content network ad placements.

The Adcenter campaigns were a home run. Over a few months time they produced around a 120% return on investment. So over one quarter, I spent approximately $6,000 to make back $13,200—a net profit margin of $7,200. This was just from one Adcenter campaign.

The revenue the Google campaign produced was about the same, only the margins were not as exciting. The Google margin was 33%, which is great for only marketing a front end sale structure on an 800 pound gorilla type market as competitive as Google.

So needless to say, for every $2,000 spent on Google, the cash inflow was around $3,000 on the front end. More on the "front end vs. back end" in (Chapter 37: On Sales Process).

Adcenter has the same or similar type of metrics for each keyword:

Keywords | Ads

Performance data for: This month Start 2/1/2012 End 2/16/2012 OK

Add or edit keywords | Import keywords | More ▾ | Select columns ▾

Keywords	Status	Match type	Qual. score	Current bid (max. CPC)	Spend	Clicks	Impressions	CPA	CTR (%)	Avg. position	Conversions	Avg. CPC
credit repair	Active	Phrase	8/10	1.00	30.58	38	2,744	0.00	1.38	5.82	0	0.80
credit repair	Active	Exact	9/10	1.00	31.70	36	1,094	0.00	3.29	6.41	0	0.88
credit repair	Active	Broad	7/10	1.00	10.67	13	1,095	0.00	1.19	5.38	0	0.82
repair credit score	Active	Broad	9/10	1.00	3.86	5	341	0.00	1.47	5.73	0	0.77
best credit repair	Active	Phrase	10/10	1.00	1.94	3	81	0.00	3.70	6.41	0	0.65
repair credit score	Active	Phrase	9/10	1.00	2.23	3	22	0.00	13.64	5.09	0	0.74
credit repair attorney	Active	Exact	10/10	1.00	1.61	3	82	0.00	3.66	3.98	0	0.54
repair credit score	Active	Exact	2/10	1.00	1.53	2	67	0.00	2.99	4.69	0	0.77
repair your credit	Active	Exact	9/10	1.00	1.61	2	98	0.00	2.04	5.89	0	0.81

As you can see in the screen shot above, you can get plenty of traffic from Adcenter's search partner network alone.

Keywords | Ads

Performance data for: This month Start 2/1/2012 End 2/16/2012 OK

Add or edit keywords | Import keywords | More ▾ | Select columns ▾

Keywords	Status	Match type	Qual. score	Current bid (max. CPC)	Spend	Clicks	Impressions	CPA	CTR (%)	Avg. position	Conversions	Avg. CPC
credit repair	Active	Phrase	-	0.50	31.75	98	48,135	0.00	0.20	5.37	0	0.32
repair credit	Active	Broad	-	0.50	83.22	190	11,857	0.00	1.60	4.76	0	0.44
credit report repair	Active	Phrase	-	0.50	4.85	15	5,513	0.00	0.27	3.12	0	0.32
credit repair attorneys	Active	Exact	-	0.50	40.90	138	3,946	0.00	3.50	4.25	0	0.30
repair credit	Active	Phrase	-	0.50	1.10	6	3,344	0.00	0.18	3.15	0	0.18
credit repair	Active	Exact	-	0.50	7.30	21	3,295	0.00	0.64	5.95	0	0.35
repair credit score	Active	Broad	-	0.50	8.53	20	3,015	0.00	0.66	7.06	0	0.43
credit report repair	Active	Broad	-	0.50	4.81	18	2,660	0.00	0.68	4.67	0	0.27
credit repair companies	Active	Broad	-	0.50	2.49	10	2,518	0.00	0.40	5.14	0	0.25

The second screenshot is the "search" only version of the same campaign. As you can see, I hit the nail on the head pretty good with most of the keyword quality scores. You can also see that I am only paying .60 to .80 cents on average for each keyword.

On Adwords, it would easily be triple that in keyword costs. I will admit that your quality score will not make or break your Adcenter campaign as much as on Adwords—at least, not yet. Adcenter just recently added the quality score feature into their platform.

I believe it is still in its infancy and it has not created a huge dividing line between advertisers, like with Google. On Google if you don't have a good quality score it is like treading water in the deep end opposed to standing in the shallow end.

It's an uphill battle, plain and simple.

Keeping high quality scores on Adwords is much more vital than on Adcenter. Microsoft's advertising polices are a lot less restrictive then Google's. This doesn't mean they don't have any policies in place. It just means that they tolerate more.

To my knowledge, unlike on Adwords, with Adcenter you can place a direct affiliate link in your destination URL.

***

Connecting the dots

- *The best way to succeed is to take action. Plain and simple.*
- *Adcenter is a better place to start than Adwords because they are less restrictive towards affiliates in their advertising policies.*
- *The costs and financial risk on Adcenter is lower than on Adwords.*
- *The quality score metric on Adcenter is not as vital as on Adwords, at least not yet.*

Chapter 23: On Tracking

"To be without tracking is to be throwing darts at a dartboard, blindfolded."
~Justin A. Spencer

Finally, the tracking section—one of the most important parts of the profitable business formula for pay per click. Without tracking, we could never accurately know how we are making money or how we are losing money.

ForeverProfitSystem.com (one of my course websites) has outstanding videos that show examples of what is discussed below – be sure to stop by and invest in the course if you want a more comprehensive edge.

Affiliate links have parameters and values. Here is what a standard affiliate link looks like: http://clickztrax.com/?a=2726&c=25411&s1=. This is an example affiliate link for the affiliate network Convert2Media, or C2M.

Clickztrax.com is the website address that the affiliate network has its affiliate tracking software installed. On this web address they have tons of data; all related to different affiliate offers.

Anything after the "?" is where the parameters and corresponding values to those parameters are located. Parameters can be used for a number of different things. Tracking is certainly one of them.

Study this line: http://AffiliateLink.com/?parameter=value

The parameter is the part of the tracking link that serves as a placeholder for the value. You can configure and control values of some parameters. The values can be static information or dynamic information.

Stay with me…

Let's look at the values of the parameters in the C2M's affiliate link below:

http://clickztrax.com/?a=2726&c=25411&s1=

The above link has 3 parameters, "a", "c" and "s1"

1. a = 2726 – the parameter "a" means affiliate. The value is 2726 which is my affiliate identification number.

2. c = 25411 – the parameter "c" means creative. A creative is a banner. The creative value is equal to 25411. Some affiliate networks have a separate parameter that indicates which offer the affiliate link gets re-directed to. C2M places this information inside the value of the creative (25411).

3. s1 = your control - the "s1" parameter stands for sub id 1.

You can use sub ids in two different ways. The first way is to write static information as the s1 value. Here is an example of static information (information that does not change):

s1=MyTrackingInformationGoesHere

You would substitute "MyTrackingInformationGoesHere" with stuff like:

1) Your traffic source
2) Your landing page, if you are sending the same traffic to different pages
3) Your ad and ad group

You are essentially labeling your affiliate link with trackback information. So if you get a sale you will have some indication as to which campaign led to the sale.

The second way to use this parameter is to set the value to a dynamic variable. In this case, the value would be equal to a variable that changes every time the link is clicked. In a moment, we will explore dynamic variables that you can use as parameter values.

It is important to understand that each affiliate network has different parameters that mean the same thing. For example the affiliate network Click Bank uses a "tid" as their parameter that represents the sub id and C2M uses "s1" "s2" and so on.

You can have multiple sub ids with C2M. You can place static information as the value of each sub id—you will see this in an example further below.

Other networks use the parameter "subid" as their sub id. Check out these examples.

Click Bank: http://affiliate-tracking-link.com/?**tid**=dynamic-variable-or-static-info-here
Azoogle network: http://affiliate-tracking-link.com/?**subid**=dynamic-variable-or-static-info
Convert2Media: http://affiliate-tracking-link.com/?**s1**=dynamic-variable-or-static-info

Here is an example for specifying static information into the values of the parameters.

In the below examples I am using 3 separate sub id's to break-up the information.

http://clickztrax.com/?a=2726&c=25411&**s1=TrafficSource&s2=LandingPage&s3=Ad-Text**

Here is an example of the above link filled in with real information for tracking purposes:

http://clickztrax.com/?a=2726&c=25411&**s1=GoogleAdwords&s2=LandingPage6&s3=Adgroup1ad2**

Now let's look at an example where we put a dynamic variable as the value for the parameter "s1" (subid1) for the C2M affiliate link:

http://clickztrax.com/?a=2726&c=25411&s1=#subid#

#subid# is a dynamic variable. Your affiliate network account has a resource that shows you what the dynamic variables are that you can use. Quick side note: variables are also referred to as tokens.

Every single time someone clicks on the above link, the variable #subid# will be different because it is dynamic and it changes for every click. Let's look at why this variable (token) is extremely useful.

The #subid# variable you can think of as a "click ID" because each click on the above link will change the #subid# variable and each link will tell a different story.

So when someone clicks on your affiliate link:

http://clickztrax.com/?a=2726&c=25411&s1=#subid#

If that person were to look in their browser bar they would see this:

http://www.creditreport.com/dni/default.aspx?PageTypeID=HomePage1&sc=674655&afid=&bcd=2726#subid#

The variable: #subid# will look very different in your tracking API. Let's look at my Convert2Media account (API) for one of the offers I was running 9/1/2011 – 9/30/2011:

All Campaigns | Today | Start 9/1/2011 | End 9/30/2011 | Filter | Export

Sub ID	Impressions	Clicks	Conversions	Conversion Perc...	Revenue	EPC
	0	31	6	19.4%	$156.00	$5.03
5y38r12l_1_1507	0	1	0	0.0%	$0.00	$0.00
62qgfbex_1_4945	0	1	0	0.0%	$0.00	$0.00
6j9eh3s3_1_4457	0	1	0	0.0%	$0.00	$0.00
9eey2894_1_1225	0	1	0	0.0%	$0.00	$0.00
9eey2894_1_2230	0	1	0	0.0%	$0.00	$0.00
9eey2894_1_2696	0	1	0	0.0%	$0.00	$0.00
9eey2894_1_3389	0	1	0	0.0%	$0.00	$0.00
cnw7dc0w_1_4321	0	1	0	0.0%	$0.00	$0.00
cnw7dc0w_1_4558	0	1	1	100.0%	$5.00	$5.00
CrPAdFclickHere	0	1	0	0.0%	$0.00	$0.00
CrPclickHere	0	7	1	14.3%	$28.00	$4.00
CsPAdFmakeSure	0	2	0	0.0%	$0.00	$0.00
dxxxqoxu_1_4347	0	1	0	0.0%	$0.00	$0.00
fbs2svta_1_1700	0	1	0	0.0%	$0.00	$0.00
fbs2svta_1_3264	0	1	0	0.0%	$0.00	$0.00
i1p73l5c_1_500	0	1	0	0.0%	$0.00	$0.00
i1p73l5c_1_5166	0	1	0	0.0%	$0.00	$0.00
kmj00ora_1_4333	0	1	0	0.0%	$0.00	$0.00
q2lvuhhe_1_2560	0	1	0	0.0%	$0.00	$0.00
*	**0**	**75**	**8**	**10.7%**	**$189.00**	**$2.52**

In the sub ID column you can see some statically assigned sub ids and some dynamic values that the #subid# became. The ones that are actually human readable are the statically assigned sub ids.

Let us look at it this way. If you send 1,000 people through your affiliate link, those 1,000 people have different stories.

- They live in different places in the world.
- They have different IP Addresses and different (ISP's) Internet Service Providers.
- They have different web browsers (Internet Explorer, Mozilla Firefox, Google Chrome, Safari).
- They have different operating systems (Windows, Mac OSX, Linux).
- They may have found your affiliate link because of Google, Yahoo, Bing or a different referral.
- They have likely used a different search query, like "Credit Report Free" or "Credit Report Fast" to find the affiliate link in your pay per click ad.
- They have likely clicked on one of many of your ads.
- They have likely landed on one of your many landing pages.
- They may have viewed more than one page on your site.
- They may have purchased an item or submitted their contact details in a form.

There is no way for us to know all of this information. We cannot statically assign sub id values to one link that meets all of these criteria for 1,000 different people. The dynamic variable #subid# stores all of this information (above). It takes the history in the person's browser and it turns it into measurable tracking data.

The #subid# variable starts recording this information as soon as the link that contains the variable is clicked.

So the token #subid# contains all of this information. Think of the #subid# as a present or gift and when you open it up, you find all these nice items inside.

These are other optional variables you can put as the values of your s1, s2, s3, etc. parameters. The sub id parameters can hold these tokens, and the affiliate network's tracking software will recognize and interpret all of this information.

Let's look at another affiliate link with other variables that are passed into it.

Note these variables are "static" variables because they will simply track back the same information—the #subid# variable is dynamic because it tracks back different information each time as discussed above.

Let's look at this example:

http://clickztrax.com/?a=2726&c=25411&s1=#subid#&s2=#oid#&s3=#affid#

http://clickztrax.com/?parameter=value

Tokens

Token Name	Token Label
#leadid#	Lead ID
#affid#	Affiliate ID
#oid#	Offer ID
#campid#	Campaign ID
#cid#	Creative ID
#s1#	Sub ID 1
#s2#	Sub ID 2
#s3#	Sub ID 3
#s4#	Sub ID 4
#s5#	Sub ID 5

Notice in the screenshot that there are variables the look like the sub id parameters. For example s5=value where sub id 5's value is your variable or static info.

What is the variable #s5# then? Simple—you can customize your own variables. So the sub ids act as place holders and as variables. A placeholder is the parameter and the variable is the dynamic info or info that the variable goes and fetches.

So the purpose of those extra tokens would be to fetch a piece of information that Convert2Media does not already provide with the tokens they have available.

What kind of information could you set your variable up to go find? I'm honestly not sure—perhaps the shoe size of our web surfers (guess we have to use our imagination).

Now let's talk about how your affiliate tracking link will interact with a conversion tracking pixel. When your affiliate link is clicked, a cookie will be placed in the web browser of whoever clicked on your link, with two exceptions.

1) If the persons web browser cookies are disabled
2) If your affiliate tracking link has a non-cookie based tracking system

Normally, upon the link being clicked, a cookie, which is simply a piece of code that tracks your website activity based on what you do in your search browser, will be activated.

Depending on the affiliate tracking link, the cookie will stay in the person's browser until manually removed or overwritten or if it expires. Cookies can last from a few days to a year, if that is how they are coded.

Most affiliate programs will not give credit to two referrers. So if someone clicks on your affiliate link then does not buy and clicks on someone else's affiliate link (for the same offer) a week later, then the second person will get credit because their cookie will have overwritten yours for that one person, specifically.

Now we understand how an affiliate tracking link works. So how do tracking pixels work?

I like to use a baseball analogy. Think of an affiliate link as the "pitcher". Think of the tracking pixel as the "catcher". When the pitcher throws the baseball to the catcher, there are 3 possibilities:

1) The batter hits the ball.
2) The pitcher throws a ball.
3) The pitcher throws a strike.

When you send people through your affiliate link (when they click on it), you are throwing a fastball at your tracking pixel.

If the person you sent through your link makes a purchase then your affiliate link threw a strike, and your tracking pixel (the catcher) caught it, and he can confirm that you got a strike.

If the batter hits the ball, then your team would be more likely to lose. In our case, we are losing money because we are not getting sales or leads from our traffic (pitches).

If the pitcher throws a ball, the traffic source has to be adjusted so we can start throwing strikes to get sales instead of balls, which are bad traffic sources or bad keywords.

You can also think of it as a basketball player who is on the foul line getting ready to shoot a foul shot. He can make it, miss it, or have a stroke and never shoot the ball (I would hope that would never happen, but it is a possibility).

He throws the basketball and your affiliate link is clicked. If the basketball goes in, then you got a sale and the rebounder (which is your tracking pixel) can confirm that the ball went in the hoop.

If he misses it, then no sale/conversion is made, and his team does not get points. He needs to re-adjust his shot and try again. Likewise, we need to re-adjust our campaign and try to make a shot or get a sale.

Installing Tracking Pixels

When you install a tracking pixel, this means you are copying your ad platform's conversion pixel and you are pasting it onto the "thanks for buying my product" page. So, the pixel is placed on the page that the person is redirected to after he/she buys.

If you are selling your own products, then you will place the conversion pixel on your "thank you for doing whatever you just did" page.

Once again, this will depend on what you are trying to accomplish— whether you are gathering leads or trying to make sales.

Put the conversion pixel on your "thank you for buying" or "thanks for your info" pages.

Once the person has that "thank-you" page served to their web browser, the conversion pixel is supposed to fire back to your Application Protocol Interface (API). This is your tracking system's dashboard or the place you login to to check your stats.

So this is equivalent to looking at your stats by logging into your Adwords or Adcenter accounts. If you do not own the offer – if you are sending traffic through your affiliate link to sell somebody else's stuff for a share of the profit, then you will email your conversion pixel to your affiliate network manager and they will place the code on the proper page that indicates you have made a sale or created a desired action such as a lead.

I usually use 5 tracking systems for my pay per click advertising campaigns. Why?

Data is money and money is data. Let that sink in. You get data by tracking. You get good data with multiple opinions, when you have multiple tracking systems in place.

Without knowing where your gems and little gold nuggets are, you will have a tough time succeeding online. Even Robert Downey Junior's' brilliant mind needed data to materialize his bold deductions in the Sherlock Holmes movies.

I use the following tools to track my websites for pay per click and search engine optimization.

1. Statcounter Pay per click and search engine optimization
2. Prosper202 Pay per click only
3. HasOffers Pay per click only
4. GetClicky Pay per click and search engine optimization
5. Google Analytics Search engine optimization only

Each tracking platform gives me different data—not different types of data. They all provide the same type of data, clicks, traffic sources, conversion rates etc. But they all read differently across the board. There is no perfect tracking system.

Cake marketing is the affiliate tracking platform industry leader; however it costs $1,500 per month to lease the software.

That is why I use all of them. The best way to make an informed decision is to know as much as you possibly can about whatever it is you are making a decision about.

I apply this logic to any business decisions I make and especially my tracking.

What types of information should you be looking for inside these tracking systems?

The details you will want to look for are the combinations of ads, keywords and landing pages that resulted in a desired action. This process is similar to trying to arrange invisible puzzle pieces together to see what fits.

This is why tracking is so important, because you will never learn where these invisible puzzle pieces are unless you are tracking, and you will surely not be able to make the pieces fit together when you are running blind.

Stuff that I look for:

1. What keywords led to a sale or lead?
2. What landing page(s) led to a sale or lead?
3. What ad led to a lead?
4. What ad placement led to a lead?
5. What combination of the above 4 created a sale or lead? (LP, keyword or ad placement, traffic source and text ad)

For example – the following combination could have led to a sale:

1. AdGroup2 & Ad text 1
2. Keyword = Free Credit Report Fast
3. Landing Page 4
4. Traffic Source =Yahoo Search

Tracking is **king**.

Setting up your tracking correctly will shed light on what is working and what is not, and you can then make changes to do better.

***

Connecting the dots

- *Affiliate links have parameters and values.*
- *You can customize the values of some parameters for tracking.*
- *You can insert static information as your parameter value for sub ids or a dynamic variable as the value for a sub id parameter.*
- *Some variables are static and simply go and fetch the same information. These variables exist because sometimes those static variables change. For example, an affiliate offer payout could change, at which point you would not have to go back to update your affiliate link, unlike statically assigning the payout info to your a sub id parameters value.*
- *Affiliate links put cookies in web browsers when they are clicked on. If the cookie finds the conversion pixel then a conversion is posted in your affiliate network's tracking API.*
- *Finding a winning combination of keywords + ads + landing pages + traffic sources will tell you outright what works.*
- *Understand tracking and you will understand how to make profitable pay per click businesses.*

Chapter 24: On Prosper202

"The more you know, the less you are surprised."
~Justin A. Spencer

Let's go through each of the 8 steps to setting up a pay per click campaign in Prosper202. This is assuming you got this baby downloaded and installed onto one of your domain names. Even if you haven't loaded it up yet, don't worry, you can still go through the run through now and always refer back to this later.

Step #1 – Traffic Source Account Setup

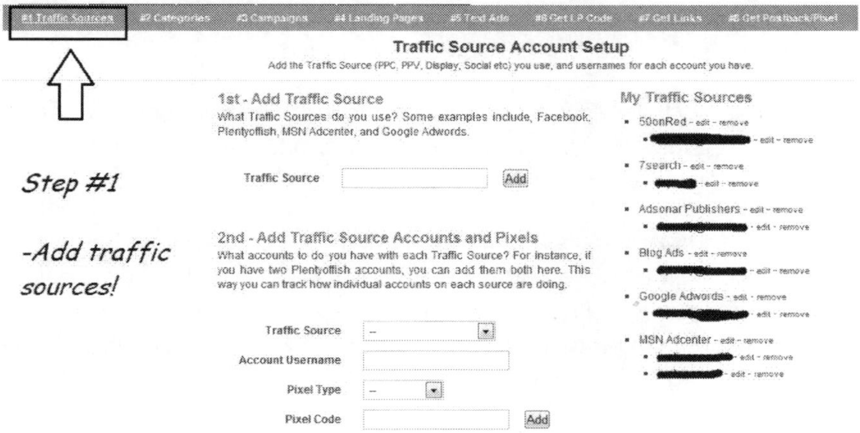

The purpose of step 1 is to add your traffic sources to your Prosper202 account. If you plan on advertising with multiple pay per click networks, you can specify where the traffic is coming from, so when you have multiple campaigns in your account later on you will easily be able to tell them apart.

Also, you might decide to send multiple traffic sources to just one of your websites which would constitute having multiple campaigns in your Prosper202 account.

Yes, there are many pay per click ad networks. You do not have to stick with just Google Adwords and Microsoft Adcenter. The sky is the limit. Just remember why Google/Yahoo/Bing traffic works better: the traffic is high quality because search traffic is interested traffic.

Not all pay per click ad networks are search traffic. Most are basically “content network” pay per click platforms. So you can select placements, much like the pay per click traffic sources listed in my Prosper202 account screenshot—707search, 50onRed, Adsonar etc.

Those are not search-based pay per click platforms, they are content networks. So the first part of step 1 is to add the traffic source so you organize your campaigns and indicate where the traffic is coming from.

For the next part of step 1, you add the username to the traffic source you previously indicated. The reason for this is if you have multiple Microsoft Adcenter accounts, for example. Then you can specify which campaign is running out of which account for that traffic source.

For the next two fields, pixel type and pixel code, you can specify what type of conversion pixel your traffic source network uses and you can copy the exact pixel into your user account.

On Google and Microsoft's advertising platforms, each network has a tracking pixel. When a web browser notices a page with this pixel on it, the pixel will "fire" and tell either Google or Microsoft (depending on which pixel is fired) that you just made a sale for a particular keyword search term that you are receiving traffic from.

Step #2 – Campaign Category Setup

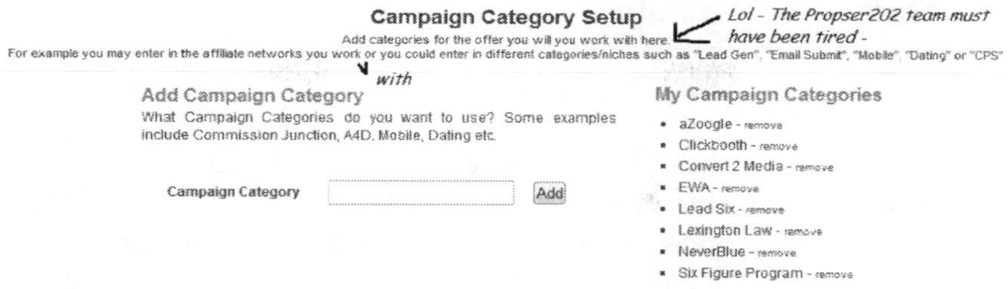

This step is pretty straightforward. Just add the affiliate networks you work with and you can categorize the offers into categories like "Lead gen" or "Mobile" as shown in the next screenshot. I just simply add the affiliate networks I work with.

Step #3 – Add a Campaign

For step 3 you want to place your affiliate URL into above field and make sure to add the dynamic sub id variable that Prosper uses, which is:

[[subid]], as opposed to Convert2Media's sub id variable, which is #subid#. Place the [[subid]] dynamic variable right after your sub id parameter. If you don't have an affiliate URL because you own the product, then simply put your landing page in the input field:
http://YourLandingPage.com/?subid=[[subid]]

Make sure cloaking is on by default. Without cloaking on, the person you are sending traffic to can see where which traffic sources you are using to make them money, along with which keywords and other information you are using to make them money when you refer sales. Why should they keep you around when they can steal your campaign and take all the profits? Leave cloaking on and they will not know where your traffic is coming from.

If you want, you can add the variables [[c1]] [[c2]] etc, and your link would like: http://Affiliate-URL.com/?s1=[[subid]]&s2=[[c1]]&s3=[[c2]]

Your sub id placeholders (parameters) can hold the other variables. You will define what the variables are in step 7.

The reason you would want to do this at all is to save time. Say you have your Prosper202 tracking link (which you get in step 7) in let's say 30 different ads, and your payout changes for that affiliate offer. Let's say the variable [[c1]] is = 28.00 because that is the commission for a sale for this particular offer. If we get a payout bump so that our new payout is 30.00, we want to reflect that in our Prosper202 account stats.

Instead of going and finding all of tracking links to change each tracking link, we can simply include the variable [[c1]] in the tracking link and update the value of c1 to 30.00 in our Prosper202 account, and the change will be reflected across all of our links. Big time saver!

As a random side note, for Convert2Media, the sub id place holder is indicated by s1 or s2 or s3. With most networks the sub id place holder is usually: sid or subid.

Examples:
http://Affiliate-URL.com/?sid=[[subid]]
http://Affiliate-URL.com/?subid=[[subid]]

<u>Step #4</u> – Landing Page Setup

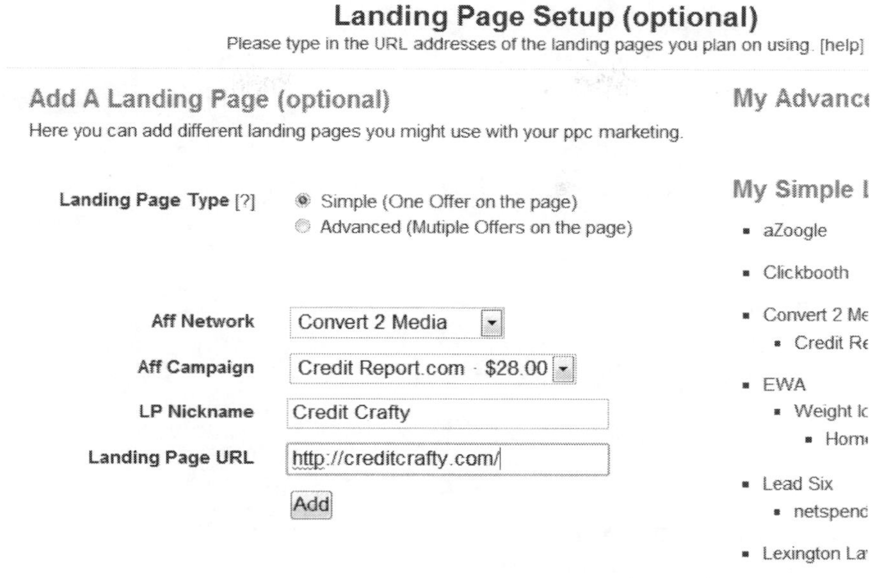

For step 4 you simply specify the affiliate network, the campaign we just configured in step 3, a landing page nickname and the landing page URL.

You can skip this step if you are not sending the traffic to a landing page, meaning you are sending the traffic directly to the affiliate offer.

Step #5 – Add Your PPC Text Ads

The point of step 5 is to add in all of your pay per click text ads so that you can track any given conversion right down to which add led to the conversion.

I only do step 5 occasionally because if I have 15 ad groups in just one pay per click campaign, then loading 30 ads into Prosper could take a while…not to mention having to create 30 separate tracking links, one for each ad, that you would then have to plug in to your ad network.

Step #6 – Setup a Simple Landing Page

In step 6 you indicate which campaign you want to get the landing page tracking code for, so fill out the necessary information from the dropdown bars and click "generate tracking link".

The next thing you will see is this:

This code is supposed to be only placed on the first page(s), that an incoming PPC visitor would be sent to. Tracking202 is not designed to be a webpage analytics, this is specifically javascript code only to track visitors coming in.

```
<script language="JavaScript" type="text/javascript">
cbr202=Math.random()*10000000000000000;document.write('<scr'+'ipt
language="JavaScript"
src="http://jmatrax.com/tracking202/static/landing.php?
lpip=9382&202cb='+cbr202+'" type="text/javascript"></scr' + 'ipt>');
</script>
```

Code A

Option 1: Landing Page: Outbound PHP Redirect Code: This is the php code so you can cloak your affiliate link. Instead of having your affiliate link be seen on your outgoing links on your landing page, you can have your outgoing links just goto another page on your site. which then redirects the visitor to your affiliate link

So for example, if you wanted to have yourdomain.com/redirect.php be your cloaked affiliate link, on redirect.php you would place our outbound php redirect code. When the visitor goes to redirect.php with our outbound php code installed, they simply get redirected out to your affiliate link.

You must have PHP installed on your server for this to work!

```
  // Tracking202 PHP Redirection, created on Fri Feb, 2012
  //
  // This PHP code is to be used for the following landing page.
  // http://creditcrafty.com/
  //
  // ----------------------------------------------------------------

  if (isset($_COOKIE['tracking202outbound'])) {
        $tracking202outbound = $_COOKIE['tracking202outbound'];
  } else {
        $tracking202outbound =
'http://jmatrax.com/tracking202/redirect/lp.php?
lpip=9382&pci='.$_COOKIE['tracking202pci'];
  }

  header('location: '.$tracking202outbound);

?>
```

Code B

The purpose of Code A is to track your referrers. So if you are sending search partner traffic and content network traffic to your landing page, you want to place Code A on your landing page and on your landing page only.

If you place Code A on more than one page of your site by accident, then the pixel will keep looking at the new referrer page, which will be a different page on YOUR site. It does not do us much good if we do not know where the person originally came from, so place Code A on the first page the person lands on, and that's it.

The purpose of Code B is to change how your affiliate link looks if someone were to scroll over it. So what you can do is copy Code B and paste into a file called: Recommendations.php and then you upload the new PHP file onto your website. Your new affiliate link is: YourLandingPageURL.com/Recommendations.php

Make sense? Instead of the person hovering over your affiliate links and seeing this in their browser:
http://YourAffiliateURL.com/?s1=[[subid]]&s2=[[c1]]&s3=[[c2]]

They would see this:
http://YourLandingPageURL.com/Recommendations.php

The 2nd optional code (Code B is optional) is Code C which is not visible in the screenshot. Code C would be java-script code instead of a PHP code like Code B. So if you wanted, you could add java-script tags to Code C to send affiliate link click-thru information back to the API of the traffic source (optional).

Step # 7 – Generating Your Tracking Links

Step 7 is pretty straightforward. This step involves specifying your campaign information so that your pay per click tracking link can be generated for this campaign. If you do step 5, (adding the text ads) then this step will take a while because you have to generate a different link for every single text ad.

When you are done filling out the drop-downs, click the button!

Here is the next screen you will see it will pop under your current screen as soon as you click the button:

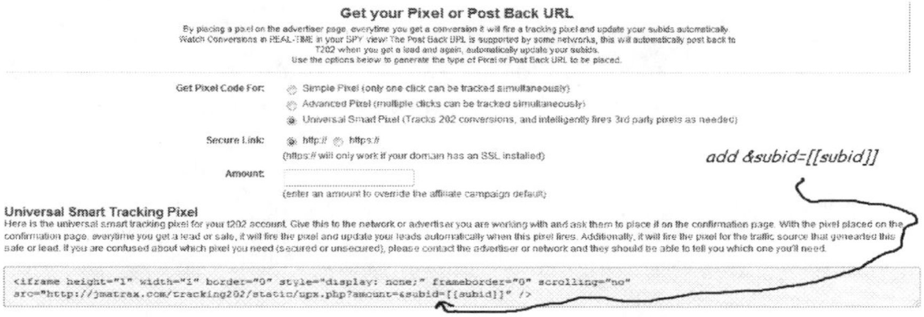

You will have to add the dynamic keyword variable {keyword} onto the end of the parameter t202kw= if you want to pass the keyword search query to your URL.

Remember, the search query will trigger the ad that contains this link, and this variable then becomes the keyword. If the keyword is greater than one word then spaces in the keyword query will be substituted with percentile characters.

So the idea for this example campaign here is to have someone go to CreditCrafty.com and click on my affiliate link that we configured in step 3, which contains the sub id variable.

Step #8 – Grab your pixel!

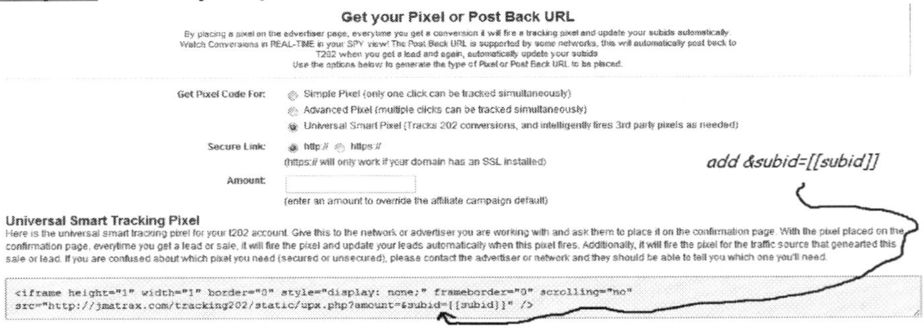

This is where we decide on a pixel, and then we paste the pixel on the "thank you for buying whatever you just bought" confirmation page. So with this campaign, I would contact my affiliate manager Susan at Convert2Media and ask her to paste the above code on the confirmation page of the CreditReport.com affiliate offer.

I just realized there is something wrong with the above pixel! The parameter a.k.a the placeholder for my [[subid]] variable is subid= it should be s1= because the Convert2Media network uses s1 as a parameter and not subid.

So the correct pixel source should be:

http://jmatrax.com/tracking202/static/upx.php?amount=&s1=[[subid]]

There are 3 different kinds of tracking pixels you can use. They are pretty self-explanatory. I normally use the universal smart pixel shown in the above screen shot. It is an iframe based pixel. Postback pixels work well too, if not better than iframe's.

***

Connecting the dots:

- *Prosper202 is an amazing and free pay per click tracking software*
- *Practice setting up a few campaigns and get familiar with the steps. The data Prosper202 gives you is substantial and you can build tons of profitable pay per click campaigns using it*

Part 4: On Email

Chapter 25: What is Email Marketing?

"The money is in the list."
~Every successful email marketer

Email marketing is simply the process of selling products/services or information to people who have signed up to be on your emailing list. Whenever you send an email, you can choose to send it to every single person who is a member of your email list.

Email marketing is absolutely fundamental for doing online business because with email, you can create and nurture a strong relationship with the people on your list who read your emails. This offers you a great chance to provide substantial value to your list and it allows the people on your list to do business with you, over and over again.

Setting up your emailing list

Here is a diagram that displays how an emailing list manager works.

Opt-in Form

The opt-in form usually contains two input text fields where the user specifies what their first name and email address is. Once the person enters in their name and email and clicks the button that is normally located right under the email field, the opt-in form will then add that person's information to the email list.

Email List

The email list itself is simply a compilation of names and email addresses.

This will be based on the opt-in form configurations. So if for example the form has more than two fields— it has fields that ask for a zip code or your last name or phone number—then all of this information can be posted to your email list for marketing or other purposes.

Auto-Responder

The auto-responder will be associated with a list. You can have multiple auto-responders and you can have multiple lists. The idea of an auto-responder is to basically put your email marketing into automation. What you can do is load up an email sequence of 10 or 100 emails, then indicate which email you would like to send out for each day, relative to when the person joined the list.

So if you have 10 emails in your auto-responder, you can indicate that you want to email the list associated with that auto-responder once a day for 10 days with your 10 pre-written emails.

Whenever you sign up with a new emailing list manager here are the steps you need to take to get your email marketing account/campaign set up. This is a basic guideline, but it will help if you wrap your mind around which steps are logically supposed to come first.

The first thing you have to do is set up a "campaign". Inside the campaign you will have to specify the following information:

- The "from" email address (JohnDoe@YourWebsiteDomain.com)
- The "from" name (John Doe)
- A physical address (to comply with the CAN-SPAM Act)

The above information will be listed on every email associated with that campaign. So any list that is associated with that campaign with have the above pre-configured information.

Here are the next steps:

1. Create a list and specify which campaign it is associated with
2. Create your opt-in form and specify which list the opt-in form posts the data to
3. Create an auto-responder and specify which list the responder will be sending emails to and on what day

Sounds pretty straight forward right? Well, it sounds easier than it is in application. But once you have the basic concept down, it gets simple with practice.

I will use aliases for my "from name" and normally I will be vague, but give a general indication of my partial physical address. I never give out precisely where I live for the physical address part—the CAN-SPAM Act simply requires you to specify a location.

You have a few options for setting up welcome emails. You can send someone a welcome email after they click the "submit" button in the opt-in form to join your list—this is called an opt-in form welcome message.

Or you can create a welcome message that gets sent out whenever someone new is added to one of your lists, based on them being added to a specific list. So the list, in a sense, sends out a welcome email—not the opt-in form.

The third option is to have the auto-responder that is attached to the list send out an email the same day a person is added to the list.

It is important to understand these 3 options. Let's look at some different situations.

Situation 1: Let's say you only want serious people joining your list, meaning you want to do a "double-confirmation" before they are added to your list. The best way to do this is to add a welcome message by means of the opt-in form. So when the person opts-in to your list—before they are added to your list—they have to go to their inbox and click on a link inside the email they received from you.

This is called a confirmation link and the person who clicks on it is acknowledging that they want to join your list.

Then it is appropriate to immediately deliver the information you said you would give to this person to get them to sign up to your list in the first place (this marketing aspect will be discussed more in the next chapter). Now it is appropriate to have the next welcome email be sent out by your list message.

This means this message is immediately sent out when someone confirms and is successfully added to the list. Then the auto-responder can dish out emails starting with one day after they signed up to be on the list, so the person gets one email per day accordingly.

Situation 2: Let's pretend we do not want them to "double opt-in" or we do not want to send them a confirmation email. Then we can skip the form welcome message and just add a list welcome message. After they fill out the form and click "submit", they should be successfully added to your list (provided they filled out the form right) and they will immediately get your welcome email.

Then the auto-responder will be set up and ready to deliver the emails to them on a day-to-day basis.

Situation 3: One last thing you could do is ignore the opt-in form and list welcome messages and just tell your auto-responder to send out the first email in the sequence the day the person joins the list.

I have done that before, for simplicity's sake, but it creates a few problems. The auto-responder guarantees the email will be sent out the same day, but it doesn't guarantee when.

Normally when someone opts in to list, they are looking for something right away, so for the sake of timing, I would refrain from using this last method.

Broadcasts

Broadcasting is when you send out an email to your entire list at once. Instead of sending out emails to each person based on the auto-responder sequence and how long they have been a member of your list, you can send out an email on the fly to everyone on your lists.

You can schedule your broadcast emails, so you can decide which time of day and day of week you want the email to hit your list subscriber's inboxes. You can also specify which people on which list(s) you want to send the broadcast to. This is in case you do not want to send a broadcast to someone who has not made it through your auto-response sequence because the email may not apply to them.

Here are a few companies who provide email list management services:

- iContact – http://icontact.com
- Get Response – http://GetReponse.com
- aWeber – http://aweber.com
- Constant Contact – http://constantcontact.com

As of writing this, I have chosen to use iContact, but I have accounts with all four of these companies, so I tried all of them. You will need to decide for yourself which company you prefer. I have heard bad stories with all four companies from my colleagues who have had email deliverability issues, support issues, their lists being locked, all kinds of stuff.

So the golden rule of thumb here is to always back up your data, meaning make copies of your auto-responder emails, broadcasts, your list(s) data, etc. In case you need to migrate to a different company, always prepare for problems. Always have a plan B.

***

Connecting the dots

- *An opt-in form transmits the user data to a list.*
- *A list is usually made up of names and emails.*
- *An auto-responder sends an email sequence to a list, over time.*
- *Broadcasts allow you to reach everyone on your list(s) at once.*
- *Email marketing is powerful. More on that soon.*

Chapter 26: Building a List

"Constructively building a list is the art of selling at its best."
~Justin A. Spencer

Building your list is as much of an art as marketing to your list. The same basic marketing logic applies when you are building a list. Here is the magical formula for successfully creating a solid list—it sounds so simple, it's embarrassing. However, executing the formula is a whole other animal.

List building formula = compelling offer + quality traffic source

Okay, now let's view what this formula actually means, through the lens of someone who has the experience and know-how to execute it. Yes I just tooted my own horn.

Anyway, here is a more detail-oriented idea of what needs to take place in order to get your list building campaign well under way.

Action step list:

1) **What is your offer?** This is the most important part of building a list. You have to sell the person on an idea or product/service or something of significant value in order for them to give you their contact information. You want to make them an offer only an idiot would refuse. Here are some examples of headlines you can use on an opt-in page also known as a squeeze page that would be highly effective:

"Give Me 2 Minutes and I Will Show YOU How I Make $547/day Using the Internet"

Fill out your name and email in the form below to get instant access!

The above headline gives something of extraordinary value to the person; you are willing to divulge a secret for making thousands per month simply for a name and email address.

Let's say you have a different offer. Let's look at some other examples:

"Learn How to Lose a Pound a Day Without Changing Your Diet or Exercising"

Fill out your name and email in the form below to learn how.

The above is a classic weight loss example. I'm curious myself about how to lose weight without changing my diet or exercising! I don't know if there is a way besides taking pills that kill your appetite, however it sounds very compelling! This is what you want to shoot for.

"Give Me Your Attention for 7 Seconds and Learn How I Make the Best Cookies on the Planet with This Secret Recipe"

Now once again, I'm even getting excited by these headlines I'm writing, because if you like cookies like I do or cooking/baking in general, then this appeals to you! Heck this should appeal to you if you are from Mars—who wouldn't want to know how to make the best cookies on the planet?

I wouldn't bake them because that's damaging to my masculinity, however I wouldn't mind telling that one girl to do it for me so I can have a 4'oclock in the morning snack.

So all in all, the message is: Have a great offer.

2) **The webpage** you need is called a squeeze page. This is a website template that has one function: to make a compelling offer to the individual looking at the page in exchange for their name and email address.

Or you will have to buy a Wordpress plug-in like Authority Pro 2. This is assuming you are not a graphics designer or a programmer. If you do not dabble in programming or graphic design, you will need to understand how to hire others to do what is not your specialty.

I personally know how to use Adobe Photoshop because I taught myself how to use it. I recommend you do the same. Once you have a basic comprehension of Photoshop you can design your websites to look exactly how you see fit. Then you can hire a programmer to take the image that you produced from Photoshop and they will then convert it to a programming language such as HTML or PHP.

I'm not going to pretend this part of the phase is easy because when you first start out, developing your websites is the biggest barrier. I know from personal experience from people whom I have given private coaching. It is unanimous that most who struggle have little or zero technical background, so obviously it helps to have some technical know-how.

It is hard to be an electrician when you know nothing about circuitry, and don't count on succeeding in real estate if you do not understand property tax laws or zoning.

You do not need to know a single line of HTML to be an exceptional internet marketer/online entrepreneur. However, it doesn't hurt know a little bit about your trade, since our primary focus as online business owners is creating websites.

What you will need to succeed is exceptional management skills. You will need the ability to understand what needs to be done, so first you will have to identify your obstacles, goals and make a blueprint or step-by-step model to follow much like this one.

You will need a basic understanding of the technical aspects in the sense of "how they work" so you can effectively create a blueprint. If you understand what needs to be done, you can then, with minimal time and energy exertion on your part, hire someone to take care of the baby steps of constructing your website for you.

Step 2 recap: (building your website)

Identify your options

1. <u>Option1</u> could be to learn how to use a product like Authority Pro to create squeeze pages.

2. Option2 could be to hire someone to create a squeeze page for you and you can describe what you want it to look like.
3. Option3 is doing a little bit of old school, getting some classic self education and learning how to do a few technical things to expand your brainpower while saving money on paying others.

3) **The list configuration** - Hire someone who is competent with your emailing list manager's API (Application Protocol Interface). They will take your opt-in code (the Javascript version or HTML version) and integrate it with your website, so that someone who opts-in with your form is correctly added to your list.

The other option is to learn how to program with PHP (pre-hypertext-processing). I always hire someone to do this simple step for me, always.

4) **Split-Testing** You will discover that certain button colors or button call to actions like "get instant access" or "sign me up today!" or "Make Money Today" will greatly change your opt-in rate. This is equivalent to a conversion rate. You will want to send the traffic through multiple pages (variations) of each type of page. You can do this by simply applying a rotation script, that redirects each person to one of 3 pages where you can then measure the opt-in rates to determine which page is the winner.

You can get a free script rotation file here.

5) **Testing traffic** - Getting an opt-in is like getting a "lead" or "conversion", so the same principles talked about in the pay per click part of this book still apply. I know from experience that it is much easier to send traffic to your squeeze page from Yahoo/Bing then it is with Google. You can imagine how unbecoming Google is about sending people to a one page website without much real content with the purpose of only collecting their personal information.

Yeah, you can bet it's not that hot. So Adcenter is a great place to start. Also Adsonar is not a bad place to check for quality traffic either. Use your imagination though; you can get plenty of list subscribers for free via Youtube and Facebook.

Do you have friends? I'll bet you do! Even if you never talk to them, make a status update or subscription channel message and tell everyone to join your list.

Following the 5 steps above will allow you to catapult yourself towards successfully building a highly targeted list of prospects.

***

Connecting the dots

- *Like anything new, building your first list will be challenging. Identifying the components of building a list will give you a much greater direction and understanding for executing the process successfully.*
- *Take time to plan the process. The more time spent planning and understanding the process, the greater chance you will have for success. The opposite is also true.*
- *Follow the 5 principles laid out above: 1) Make an Offer 2) Plan Your Site 3) Configure the List 4) Test Your Website 5) Test & Track Your Traffic*

Chapter 27: Marketing and Building Trust with Your List

"When dealing with people, remember you are not dealing with creatures of logic, but creatures of emotion."
~Dale Carnegie

Connecting with your list subscribers on an emotional level will cultivate a strong bridge of trust between them and yourself.

Building trust and credibility with your list will open many doors for not only you, but for your list as well. By engaging your list with emails that are sincere, honest and value-based, they will allow you to build a great reputation for yourself.

Trying to connect with people on your list based on similarities and personal stories is an excellent strategy. Depending on what type of expert you are, based on your niche, every now and then people love to know that you share the same experiences as them.

For instance, I recall Donald Trump talking about this in his book, Think like a Champion. Plain and simple: letting people know that you have to deal with the same hocus pocus stuff will bring them closer to you.

Most people experience traffic jams, flight delays, have had a headache or have been nervous. When you explain these things to your list they feel like they can relate to you and they will trust you.

You can share personal stories about how your dog is going through the bathroom-training process and compare it to something else relevant in your niche that is a pain in the neck! Once you show your list that you are a human too, they will have a better connection with you.

Why is building trust and reputation so important when you are emailing your lists? People will be more inclined to do business with you if they trust you. This is not a mystery, but many who try email marketing are shortsighted and have a tough time getting the subscribers on their list to buy from them because they have not established that bridge of trust with their list.

Another great way to build trust with your list is to deliver on your promises. This will earn you a unique reputation for being reliable which is another route to trustworthiness.

Keep in mind; you are still competing to get the attention of the people who signed up to be on your list. Just because they have expressed interest in what you have to share with them does not mean that you are not on the list of 80 other people who are also sending crud to their inbox.

You have to be exceptional. Just like anything in business, if you want to stand out and truly excel and be successful you have to separate yourself from the competition.

You can do this by being straight-forward with people and by truly providing something of value to your list. If you can do this, you will have gained an asset far greater than 99% of anything you own.

A list is equivalent to a very large group of people who have a special interest in what you are trying to sell to them. It is equivalent to being at an online auction.

The power of a list built on trust is indispensable. Let's put this into perspective with other forms of getting customers. In this book, we have discussed how to get traffic so that we can transform searchers into customers from search advertising. We can turn our traffic sources into customers by selling someone else's product or service as an affiliate, or by selling something we have to offer.

It costs an immense amount of time and energy to do SEO and/or PPC and if we do not try to capture or retain that traffic, we are spending money on PPC or on backlinks for SEO and then we lose customers that we could have potentially had for years, if not a lifetime.

Instead of spending money every single day on your pay per click campaigns to convert new people into buyers, why not sell to customers who know you and trust you and are already willing to buy from you, again and again, at no cost to you?

When we put it into that perspective, the decision seems quite obvious. Time and energy spent building a list and developing a relationship with that list is time well spent.

Your email list is the equivalent to something coined as: “the back-end”. This means that you retain those customers by capturing their name and email instead of never seeing them again when they leave your website.

This is a key concept because it means you can afford to pay more to get new customers because you can simply make money from them at a later date. The real idea is to offer something of genuine value, perhaps at a lower cost as an upfront sale to attain a customer, because this customer may be willing to buy other products that are more fashionably priced in the future.

You will see this often in the information marketing niches. Whether the person is selling information about how to make money online, how to invest in real estate, how to make money with stocks or how to train your dog, the fact remains.

Oftentimes the goal of the producer is to “hook” the person so that he/she can build a more intimate relationship with the new customer/prospect.

To clarify: a prospect is someone who has opted in to your list but has not purchased a product/service yet, and a customer is someone who has already purchased a product/service.

The value of owning a list like this may already seem clear to you but to further extend the point let’s look at some numbers, because numbers always make the topic more comprehensible.

To get my point across, let us suppose you have taken the time to collect 100,000 names and email addresses that make up your vast list. You have earned and gained the trust of those who subscribe to you. They know you enough by know to understand that you are genuine, reliable and have integrity. Now let's say you create a product, or simply want to recommend a product to your list.

Here is where the numbers do their deed:

It takes you 200-300 seconds if you are focused, to write an objective based email explaining to your list the value in the product you are recommending or selling on your own behalf.

After 2 hours, 40% of the 100,000 (40,000) people open your email because they value your emails and opinions on things. Of those 40,000 people, let's say only 10% of them, which is an extremely conservative metric, but nonetheless, only 4,000 people click thru your product referral link (affiliate link) or your link to your sales page for your product. Let's say the product you are selling or referring earns you a small $30 per sale.

Of those 4,000 people who decided to click through, let's say that 5% of them decided to buy the product. This equates to 200 sales.

In retrospect you just made $6,000 profit for writing a 200-300 second email to your list. It is literally like opening up the floodgates of cash on demand. This was assuming that less than half your list even opened the email to begin with. Do you see where this is going?

Imagine how powerful and accomplished you would feel if you set up an SEO based business or PPC campaign that cleared $6,000 profit in one single day. Now imagine you could spend 2 minutes writing an email to your list while you're in between catching flights at the airport, making more money in mere seconds than many do in months.

Now, big numbers like 100,000 will obviously create other bigger numbers like 6k paydays, but the next point is this: you can send 100,000 hits to your website every day via PPC or SEO methods if you have a line of credit available to you for $200,000 and were able to afford such a thing. This is a bit impractical and escaping the main point, which is this: Can you imagine having 100,000 people at your fingertips every single day?

I don't think I need say more about the value of having a list. Create your own traffic sources. Do not depend on Google or Yahoo or Bing. Use them as instruments to create your own empire. Period.

***

Connecting the dots

- *Build trust to build your wealth.*
- *Add value to others' lives by sending meaningful emails and you will see the positive - mirrored effects in your own life.*
- *Use other traffic empires to create your own traffic empire, do not depend on Google, use Google as a means to your own traffic on demand source.*

Chapter 28: Joint Ventures

"Leadership is the capacity and will to rally men and women to a common purpose and the character which inspires confidence."
~Bernard Montgomery

Rally the troops! Be a leader, build an army, inspire confidence and create numbers and value on an enormous scale. Humans are creatures limited by imagination only.

Being able to profit from a list does not mean you have to own the list. There are many other information marketers who have huge lists built on trust. Many information marketers or producers who have a good product decide to team up with other marketers who have access to large lists.

Let's face it; building a high quality list takes a lot of time and money upfront. Why not leverage someone else's list by doing a joint venture with them in order to sell your own stuff and catapult your name out there to make a reputation?

A joint venture is simply "teaming up" with another marketer. This is commonly done when one marketer has a good product to sell and another marketer has a big, quality list to sell it to.

Even if you have a high quality list yourself, it still makes sense to do joint ventures. If you have a state-of-the-art product with explosive value, why not do as much business as you can? Doing as much business as you can is the point of business! The purpose of business is to increase your profits and bottom line.

So how do you get in contact with someone to do a joint venture?

A little bit of due diligence and persistence on your part will help you uncover the answers. A few practical suggestions that I do personally, is to call or email the person if they have their contact information listed or available.

If they are close geographically, it makes sense to meet up and have a face to face discussion about the venture. If they are not, then you can handle everything over the phone successfully.

Chances are that if you were able to produce your own product, then you will have enough drive to find joint venture partners. It is no different than affiliate scouting—you are essentially looking for someone to sell your product: preferably someone with a big name who has access to a big, high quality list, because list traffic is top-notch.

Common sense will usually allow you to successfully set up a joint venture with someone even if you have never met them before. Just be honest and direct.

Explain that you have an awesome product and stand by it with confidence. Offer to give the product to your potential joint venture partner at no cost, (obviously) so he/she can review it and form their own opinion as well.

If they like your style, which chances are that they will because you are reaching out to him/her to make more money for him/her as well as yourself, they then will effectively promote your product and they will likely be able to generate a large amount of sales based on how big their list is, and how good of a relationship the JV partner has with their list.

I have witnessed amazingly successful product launches before by simply being on a list of a few other avid email marketers. I saw a $47 product do over a million dollars just during the product launch itself—because of joint ventures.

The ability to scale your product when you team up with others is extraordinary. Another obvious thing you can do is get multiple joint venture partners, which is equivalent to building an army of marketers to sell your product.

You can even be so creative as to give away prizes and vacation trips to your fellow marketers who are selling your product the most!

***

Connecting the dots

- *The money is in the list.*
- *You do not need to own a list to make money with one.*
- *Partnering/joint ventures create huge income potential.*
- *Be creative and have fun with everyone you are doing joint ventures with. Who knows, no matter the outcome, you will have likely made some valuable business connections.*

Part 5: On Your Success

Chapter 29: Declare War on Normalcy

"A normal life is a life absent of excitement and saturated with contentment."
~Justin A. Spencer

Let us first talk about what it means to be abnormal. Not abnormal in the sense of being dysfunctional, but abnormal as in going against the grain. I can tell by your curiosity in our conversation that you have expressed interest in becoming the minority.

I mean: an *employer* instead of an *employee*.

This is a bold transition with bold rewards. Breaking free from the everyday norm and doing something entirely different will require your time, energy and focus. There are no shortcuts to your destination, but there are many escape routes along the way. You can choose to exit off the highway to abnormality or you can keep pushing onward.

A normal lifestyle is defined as a life that is predictable or common. You do what everyone expects you to do, you take fewer risks and rely more on certainties. The normal lifestyle expects you do follow the masses.

In America, the normal lifestyle is (or was) to go to high school, then college while working part-time, and then to graduate to get a job with a nice salary or hourly wages with benefits. Then you invest in mutual funds and an IRA or 401(k) for 40 years and retire. Sound familiar?

According to the U.S. Census Bureau, there is a population of approximately 313 million people living in the United States. There are approximately 27 million employers. If you round up, the percentage of employers is 9%, opposed to employees at 91%.

This quick calculation obviously does not take into account children who are part of the population and are not yet capable of becoming employers. It also does not take into account the self-employed who are not employers or employees.

But you see the point, if normal is thought to be common, then the common thing is to be an employee. Don't let those numbers scare you though. There has to be a strong work force in place in order to keep the businesses intact for our country's economy to function.

My point is this: you have to declare war on normalcy.

In order to be unlike most people, you need to do uncommon things. Uncommon rewards may involve going to the island Fiji for an exotic retreat, or owning your own private jet, yacht or simply having a consistent financial income stream that provides options and ultimately freedom.

In order to obtain those uncommon experiences, you need to be uncommon. You can do this by declaring war on the normal, stereotypical lifestyle. When you decide to declare war, know that there will be many battles. Some you will win, others you will lose and learn from.

Have you experienced your wildest dreams, desires, and life goals? If you have not, then you are normal.

Ask yourself right now: are you happy with your life and the path you are taking?

Do not confuse contentment with happiness. There is a crystal clear difference between being happy and being content. If you are okay with being "content" or "settled in", then you will likely lack the tenacity to become successful as an entrepreneur.

Starting a business is difficult and you must have strong motives for doing so. You may think your motives are great, but if you have self doubts and unclear motives, waging a war on the normal will become abnormally difficult. You will need to find motives to supply you with endurance on your journey, but don't worry, we will discuss this soon in (Chapter 30: On Motivation and Passion).

Here is another question to probe yourself with to figure out if you are not where you truly desire to be: do you dislike going to sleep and enjoy waking up?

If you enjoy waking up and dislike sleeping then I think you are doing what you truly love to do and I would argue that some part if not all of you is fulfilled. But let's look at the opposite: do you roll out of bed to start yet another day out of obligation?

If this is you, then it is time for a change. Life does not get easier when you get older—in fact the reverse is true. With age comes wisdom, but by default it is harder to gain the energy and vigor you once had at an earlier age.

However, do not forget it does not matter if you are 17 or 65—it is never too late to declare war on normalcy and make a change! You do not want to decide that you could have done a better job conducting your desired lifestyle when it is too late to reap the benefit of it.

Let's face it, we are on this earth for around 80 years, more or less. It makes sense to try and become rich when you are young so you can enjoy it and give back. It is ineffective to wait until you have almost exhausted your natural timeline to become rich. No one can be happy 100% of the time; however YOU can choose to be happier than 99% of other people by being abnormal.

Let's face it, life is not always going to go our preferred way. But if it did, life would also not be that interesting. So embrace your faults, your gifts, your strengths, your weaknesses, your failures and your successes. Declare war on anything average, common or normal! Empower yourself. Know that you are in control. Life is much more satisfying if you try and fail then if you do not try at all.

Bringing everything back into perspective

When you become an employer as opposed to an employee, you no longer have to rise up in the morning to satisfy an obligation. You are not required to start working on your business at 9 a.m. and you are not required to stop working on your business at 5 p.m.

When you work for a company as an employee, you subconsciously immerse yourself in that commitment because you understand the consequences of dishonoring that commitment or obligation.

When you go into business for yourself and you still have a back-up plan, which is to be an employee, I will argue that you have not fully immersed yourself or committed to your business and declaring war on the norm.

I'm not saying you cannot hold a job while you are starting or launching your business. That is to be expected because you need to be able to survive. Here is what I am saying: if you do not arrive at the decision to fully embrace, immerse and commit to your business, you will not succeed, period.

No one ever experienced exceptional results by "dabbling" in something. I don't care what you have heard or been told. Greatness is earned; it does not magically take form.

My next point is this: when you work for someone else, you immerse yourself and form a commitment to work for that person because you need the end result to survive.

When you work for yourself, you need to have the same attachment to your business. Even in my short existence so far, I have seen so many people give up on something because it did not automatically work for them.

Launching and running a successful business is not rocket science and it is NOT easy. There will be problems, every single day. The more success you have, the bigger the problems will be. Your success and your problems will grow proportionately, but luckily, so will your confidence in yourself and your ability to handle these types of problems. These problems are the residue or battles that will result after you declare war on normalcy! Your problems are opportunities dressed in disguise!

There will be many potholes in the road, and there will be great difficulty, but great problems are accompanied by great opportunities.

***

Connecting the dots

- *To declare war on normalcy is to decide to live an abnormal life. You will have abnormal experiences and abnormal achievements with each battle that you win.*
- *You cannot have abnormal rewards without an abnormal state of mind.*
- *Decide: are you truly happy? Not just content or settled in.*
- *Immerse yourself. Do not dabble in business. Dabbling in something means it is simply a hobby, not a business, and you will not get abnormal results. You need to honor a full-fledged ironclad commitment.*
- *With great success, you will be accompanied with great problems. Remember: problems are the father of opportunity.*

Chapter 30: On Motivation and Passion

"The most powerful weapon on earth is the human soul on fire."
~Field Marshal Ferdinand Foch

Early on I learned that one of my secrets to success was finding key motivators that I was very passionate about, that registered with me on an emotional level. I realized that if you can train yourself to think about something that is so overwhelming that it makes you feel like crying, or angry, or upset, then you have found a key motivator that touches you emotionally, and sparks flames of passion. Tapping into these passionate thoughts will give you energy and resolve.

When you are passionate about something, you work harder, you work longer and you have more enthusiasm. Passion will allow you to wake up with the same objective or goal you had the night before. It is human nature to be extremely ambitious one day and after we go to sleep and wake up, we feel the invisible pull to dismiss our ambition from yesterday.

By nature we desire normalcy—more specifically, we desire security. We desire sameness to a degree. The beautiful paradox is that we actually desire to desire what we actually want. But we struggle trying to find ways to stay with a consistent thought pattern and when this thought pattern is new and we don't want to let go of it, it becomes that much more difficult to retain. What motivates you one day may not motivate you the next.

You need to find a reason to achieve what you want to achieve and that reason has to be built on passion, otherwise the motivation will only be temporary.

What are you passionate about?

I understand what I am passionate about, and it has led me to where I am today. I am passionate about having free will and the ability to choose. I am also passionate about helping others. I get satisfaction and fulfillment from producing. These passions inspire me to keep working, no matter what.

Your passions will determine what you do, and what you do will determine who you are, and who you are will determine what you have the ability to become.

Earlier, when I told you about the cold winter walk that changed my life, I believe the feeling I felt that night was passion. I became aware that I had a choice and the mystic feeling that accompanied me that night and warmed me from the inside was a byproduct of passion.

I became very passionate from then on and after that night, I became passionate about redirecting and remapping the course in which my life had been going. Whenever I had no energy left, after school and work I would think about the feeling that I felt that night. Every single time, even to this day and as I write this, I become filled with the same passion. It's the overwhelming feeling that gives me energy that I did not know I possessed. Energy is the byproduct of passion.

One of my business role models, Donald Trump, said it perfectly: "Without passion you don't have energy, without energy you have nothing."

Figuring out what drives you, what moves you, will be your greatest self discovery. Your passions will motivate you and they will not burn up like ordinary desires. They will burn on after you go to sleep and wake up the next day. Your passions will defy normalcy. They will ultimately shape you, if you let them.

***

Connecting the dots

- *Passion creates energy.*
- *Energy creates action.*
- *Action creates change.*
- *Changes will shape your desired lifestyle.*
- *Ask yourself what you are passionate about.*
- *What do you live for?*
- *What brings you great joy or happiness?*

Chapter 31: On Environment and Focus

"Environment changes your physical reality and has the ability to empower or destroy you."
~Justin A. Spencer

Being in a sound environment is one of the keys to focus. If you have energy, endurance and desire, but no focus, you will not be able channel those powers in a productive manner to make things happen. Much of this book was written at different places at different times. Sometimes, when you switch the environment in which you are working, your attitude changes and your productivity frequency suddenly becomes properly tuned.

I wrote a lot of rough drafts of this book while in Starbucks. The dim chatter of the people talking around me and the infrequent banging of metal and occasional stir of the blender mixing drinks, with the soothing music in the background really just put me in the mood to work.

When you are around other people working, you can become more inclined or in the mood to work too.

Environment affects your attitude, and your attitude affects your ability to focus, and when you can focus, you can be productive in order to make progress towards your goals and objectives. When you make progress towards your goals, you feel accomplished and this further boosts your attitude in a positive tune. The process refuels itself and this why learning where or what your ideal environment is can be very beneficial.

I learned that soft music, particularly film scores, which are the soundtracks, played in movies; help form a nice working environment. The film score music also has no lyrics and this further complements my ability to focus. Writing a book is difficult if someone else is singing in the background, in my opinion.

Placing yourself in an environment that is in line with a desire or passion that you have, will further complement your ability to focus and be productive. For instance, if one of your passions or desires is to travel around the world, then pretending that you have reached your goal of becoming financially independent and self sufficient, by working in locations that create that type of aura, will further improve your attitude and your focus.

This is what I mean: if you were financially independent then you can decide where you want to work. If you choose to work in a Starbucks, a subway shop, a mall, an airport or another place like this it emits the aura that you are already financially free and it further reinforces your work ethic while giving you a taste of what it would feel like.

This is one of the reasons why I used to work at different Starbucks locations before I was financially independent. It complemented the idea that I was free and working leisurely in a nice, luxurious type of environment even though I was a broke college kid. Nowadays, I still work at Starbucks quite frequently because I still like the environment.

Ask yourself this: what type of environment do you enjoy working in?

Do you have a morning ritual you do in order to get in the mood to work? Shuffle these types of questions through you mind and determine what your most ideal work environment would be. It will be different for everyone.

I simply love the concept of working in a different location every day. It is much easier now too, since I'm beginning to travel more frequently. I know other people who are the most productive when they are at their office or their house. Whatever it may be, make sure you understand what your productive environment is, so you can harness it in order to maximize the output of your energy in the least amount of time.

Let's take a second to explore the opposite. When you are constantly in an environment cluttered with negativity and disorganization, you can expect the same effects to carry over on your focus.

It will not be easy to focus when you are not in a positive environment where you are free to think for yourself. Working in a new location every day from my laptop is very abnormal—that's what I like about it. It complements the fact that I'm being abnormal, which could be a type of subconscious assurance mechanism so it makes everything feel like I am doing the right thing.

Find your environment. If you do not know what your ideal environment is, try different locations and see if you can work with a dull buzzing in the background like in Starbucks or maybe you prefer total silence.

Either way, you can use the power of your motivational triggers in (Chapter 30: On Motivation and Passion) to further influence your energy if you cannot escape your present environment.

***

Connecting the dots

- *Environment is the key to focus.*
- *A positive environment will help you grow. A negative environment will threaten your determination and go against your goals.*
- *A positive environment is much like swimming with the current in a river and a negative environment is like swimming against it. Work smart!*
- *If you do not have the means to change your environment, focus on your internal motivators to create your drive, then propel yourself with your drive to create new, more desirable environments.*

Chapter 32: On Control

"The more a person seeks security, the more that person gives up control over his life."
~Robert T. Kiyosaki

Control is your greatest asset not only in business, but in life. Control is what separates employees from executives. Control separates the poor from the wealthy. Control determines processes, outcomes, results and events. Control determines lifestyles, happiness, fulfillment, satisfaction and purpose.

Here is the dividing line between happiness and partial happiness:

Are you in Control? | Or are you obligated?

Are you strapped to your dead end job because you have bills to pay?

Do you find yourself unhappy working 5 days a week to get a lousy 2 days off?

Did you buy the "go to college and get a job" dream that society was selling you?

Did you go right into the workforce to make money seeking financial freedom?

Are you a college graduate searching for a job?

Are you in control of your cash inflow? If you do not write your own checks, then you are not in control. If you are not in control, then you are susceptible to losing your income without fault of your own.

When you work for someone else you are an employee. When you are an employee the amount of security you have is **limited** and your options in life are **limited**.

1. You are **limited** by the hours of the day you can work
2. You are **limited** by the amount of money you get paid per hour
3. You are **limited** by your hours getting changed or cut
4. You are **limited** by your own health or sickness to show up
5. You are **limited** by location
6. The amount of money you can make is **limited**
7. Your freedom is **limited** because your options are **limited**
8. Your happiness becomes **limited**

As an employee, you will never possess true wealth, with a few exceptions.

You can work 16 hour days to climb the corporate ladder from an employee to an executive position someday, or you can become famous or become a professional athlete or win the lotto.

Unless you have natural talent and a burning desire to become a professional athlete or famous rapper, actor, comedian or entertainer then this separates the means by which you can create your wealth.

Perhaps a few of these paradoxes will help you better understand the power of control.

- You **cannot** control time; you can **control** what you do with your time.
- You **cannot** control the weather; you can **control** where you live.
- You **cannot** control the economy; you can **control** where you invest your money.
- You **cannot** control your shoe size; you can **control** the shoes you buy.

Getting what you desire out of life is about controlling what you can and using it to your advantage to work for you, instead of you working for it.

Read the above line again.

This is called leverage. Like most people who live and breathe on planet Earth, there is a great possibility that you have been indoctrinated by the common dogma that insinuates you need to work for someone else to "live the dream". The philosophy is to work 5 days a week and to throw $300.00 in your account each and every single month for 40-45 years. Excellent, that sounds like a blast! Let's be a minion and help our companies executives get that new multi millionaire dollar private jet or yacht—sign me up!

Most subscribe to the idea that "getting by" is good enough when they honestly are not aware that there is a better way. Others do desire more than getting by but they are simply not sure on how to advance this feeling into action. The lesson in this chapter is to start thinking in terms of control and leverage. Ask yourself questions: can I control this? Can I control how this starts or ends? Am I the architect, the designer, the mastermind, the author, can I control the outcomes of the decisions I am making?

Quiz yourself, answer honestly, and be active and committed to probing yourself with these types of questions.

When 90% of businesses fail in the first 5 years, why would you want to start a business instead of having the nice, gentle, warm, cushy and reliable 9 to 5 job?

If a business failed it was because the owner who established it did not do their homework or the business model did not fit the business or that it was mismanaged till the ship eventually sunk.

***

Connecting the dots:

- *Are YOU in control or are YOU obligated?*
- *Living the life you want involves controlling as many things as you have control over. You can control many things that apply to your happiness such as where you live, your income and your ability to have options.*

- *Determine what you can control now and decide how to reap the rewards.*
- *Focus on getting more things that are important in your control.*

Chapter 33: On Habits

"First we make our habits, then our habits make us."
~Charles C. Noble

Our decisions govern our habits. What we decide in any circumstance can lead to the formation of a habit. Whether it is a good habit or a bad habit varies on the ending result of the habit, or what the habit produces for us in our physical reality as a result of whatever the habit is.

Our motives or underlying thoughts and desires will craft our habits and routines. What we desire determines our choices; our choices determine our physical reality.

Items that are the cause of an inspiration can attempt to create habits that are likely for a radical purpose that is foreign to our normal habitual structure. If we find something that inspires us, we want to cultivate and nurture that feeling. We do not desire to dismiss it as soon as it comes. The attempt to create a newly discovered habit that will breed that feeling is a road filled with potholes because things that inspire us naturally require energy and focus.

The power of our very own thoughts is substantial and most are unaware of this. One particular thought can lead to a string of thoughts that develop habits that can either produce positive results or negative outcomes.

A straight A+ teenager with a naturally brilliant mind is destined for greatness until one day when he walks home from school and stumbles into a crowd of fellow teenagers smoking pot. With the pressure of the moment, the uninformed teenager smokes pot and finds it more enjoyable then pursuing his studies.

The teenager who had good habits completely demolished his previous routines to try something he was not informed about. He then forms a new habit. He becomes a bum and he depends on others to loan him money so that he can afford to buy more pot. Eventually, he is bored with smoking, so he needs to find more powerful drugs to give him a more intense feeling. He falls further astray past the point of no return when he experiments with more powerful tablets and pills.

One uncalculated choice can lead to a series of other choices and habits that will define your very existence.

A different student who also smokes pot from the same institution who has no ambition in life can also be steered back onto a more satisfying life. Let us depict his math teacher holding him back for a moment after class ends. The teacher takes a second and looks the student right in the eyes and says: “Student, you have the potential to be somebody great. I know this, and you need to start caring about who you are becoming—I believe in you.”

The feeling of hope and belief that was absent at the student’s home now fills his soul with the power of the influential teacher’s words. The student channels his energy to ambition and his ambition into focus, and he becomes someone great. The gravity of a small event can initiate a sequence or chain of events that define the very existence of a person.

Habits are so powerful because they are continuous. They are thoughts translated into actions, day in and day out. The fundamental flaw with 99% of peoples’ habits is that they are indoctrinated and built on false premises. People form habits based on the knowledge that they possess. Inarguably, you cannot form a continuous line of thoughts or actions if you are not aware that you are allowed to do so.

Our belief system either inhibits or propels us to formulate habits that we actually do desire to possess instead of digesting habits we possess that we do not care for. Perhaps one could argue that people do not go to work out of habit, but more so because they are obligated to go to work because they need money to pay their bills.

Regardless of how you see it, showing up to your 9 to 5 is a habit as much as it is an obligation because your body and mind are accustomed to waking up at the same time for at least 5 days week. Your body is accustomed to when you eat dinner because of the effect your job has on the time in which you choose to eat to begin with.

Habits are peculiar in nature because it is outlandishly hard to break free from them, yet so easy to cultivate new ones. The more we resent and fight the habit, the more the habit fights for its own survival.

If you have a habit of undermining yourself and your abilities, then trying to overwrite that habit is difficult because the mind is so accustomed to producing these thoughts.

The ability to control your thoughts is a power that is earned over time by applying discipline and conditioning. In the past and sometimes to this day, despite the fact that I'm well aware of my own mental powers, I can feel a spike in the back of my mind that exists but has faded and lost much of its power.

This spike was a negative thought that surfaced in my mind one day and I hated that the thought had ever entered my mind. I then associated an emotion with this thought, and any time I felt the emotion the thought would resurface, beckoning me further to feel discontent with myself.

I do not mean to tease you, but I will not reveal what the exact thought was. However, I will more importantly enlighten you as to what allowed me to find a cure to this poisonous spike that polluted my mind.

In computer programming, I learned a line of code in the PHP coding language that quickly re-directs a connection to another connection. The following code represents a "header re direct" which simply points to a new address from the original address that was requested: <?php header('Location: http://Send-to-this-address.com'); ?>

I applied this concept to some of my thought processes.

Whenever I feel my thoughts wandering into a direction I do not desire, I quickly "re-direct" my thoughts to something funny or comical or instrumental in getting my thoughts back to where they should be.

It's almost like tapping into a negative thought that quickly re-directs in less than a second to a positive thought. This technique has allowed me to successfully formulate habits that require more discipline.

Since habits define our physical reality, the thoughts behind these habits are the most important factor in the formula for establishing habits that create positive outcomes.

Your belief system is established by your knowledge. What you are aware of allows you to reason and form beliefs. Therefore if you are not aware that it is completely possible to be a billionaire in a year then you will not know that you can create a habitual structure that will dictate this outcome.

Here is the ultimate recipe to forming better habits.

1. Read and comprehend this book.
2. Fuel your mind with knowledge that allows you to understand the infinite possibilities that are available to you to make your fortune. You can do this by reading how others made their fortunes.
3. Reshape your belief system after you understand and have concluded that it is well in your power to become a millionaire or billionaire if you desire it.

Immerse yourself in creating new habits that support your goals and dreams. Do not just try and "dabble" in the habit creating process. It will take energy, focus, and discipline to do what you may have never done in your entire life.

***

Connecting the dots:

- *Repetitive actions become habits, whether they are positive or negative.*
- *One thought or idea can lead to a string of other thoughts or ideas that can help you tremendously or damage your mindset tremendously.*

- *When you feel a negative thought entering your mind, re-direct that thought to a positive one.*
- *Deleting old, bad habits is difficult and requires discipline. Through persistence it can be done.*
- *Read about others who have formed good habits and how they did it.*

Chapter 34: On Responsibility and Accountability

"The price of greatness is responsibility."
~Winston Churchill

Taking responsibility is as much an art as it is a habit that can be developed. If someone poked me on the shoulder and asked me my opinion on responsibility, I would likely reply something within the vicinity of: "Responsibility is a powerful and uncommon tool inherited by those who understand that their actions have led to the outcomes they have enjoyed or endured. Responsibility is also the acceptance for the circumstances or events that occur for or against our better preference."

Responsibility is easily defined yet it is not easily practiced. People are wired to have a critical response to being accused or blamed of anything. Accepting that your actions led to a poor outcome is not an ego booster; it inherently reveals a weakness in your choice or decision and ultimately makes you appear weak or flawed.

Accepting that you are not flawless is a better thought to subscribe to. Fighting your flawed human nature will be a never-ending uphill battle. A potent remedy for creating a sense of responsibility towards your actions is not to justify why you made the decision, but to openly accept the blame without making excuses. You know why you chose to do whatever is was you chose to do. Creating a sense of responsibility does not lie in explaining yourself to others. It lies in accepting the consequences of your actions.

This brings us to our next topic: Accountability.

Responsibility and accountability are like the edges of a two sided sword. In order for a sword to properly defend off attackers and contribute to winning a battle, each side of the sword needs to be primed to defend the multiple entry points of your attackers. If one side of the sword is defective then you have to twist the sword 180 degrees to strike, which creates repetitive opportunities for ambush from one side.

As with the sword, a responsible person accepts the consequences of their actions for what they are without the need for justification. However, accepting your actions does not prevent them from reoccurring. The accountable person not only accepts their actions, but they learn from them and adjust accordingly to prevent the undesired action from reoccurring.

The responsible warrior understands and accepts the fact that the defective sword he brought to battle almost got him killed. The accountable warrior learns from this and sharpens the other side of his sword so he does not expose himself to death with a defective weapon. Likewise, the accountable person remembers choices that led to desirable consequences and uses them to his advantage in the future.

There is a saying that goes something like this: "The smart individual learns from his mistakes. The wise individual learns from others mistakes." This outlines how powerful and indispensable knowledge is, generally speaking. Learning from multi-millionaires' mistakes is a great way to ensure that you do not make the same or similar mistake when you earn your fortune. Accepting your failures and faults as milestones on your journey towards success and developing successful habits is essential. Transforming a negative substance into a positive substance will have an exponentially large impact on your success.

Think of it in mathematical sense. If the power of a negative thought or habit is equal to the value of negative 2,000, this integer is determined by the affect the negative thought has on your ability to create success yielding thoughts and habits.

Imagine this integer's inverse, which would be positive 2000. The positive affect it would have on you would be enormous. My point here is that the inverse of negative 2,000 is positive 2000, which is an increase in intensity by 4,000, as opposed to shifting from 1 to 3, for example.

Likewise when you start flipping negatives to positives in your thought processes it exposes the limitless potential of things and products you can produce if you execute correctly.

When you starting transforming your thoughts from:

- "I will try" to "I will do"
- "I will look" to "I will find"
- "I will consider" to "I will start"
- "I will see" to "I will achieve"
- "I will think" to "I will produce"

***

Connecting the dots:

- *Responsibility is accepting the consequences of your decisions.*
- *Accountability is learning from your consequences so you do not make the same mistakes.*
- *Being responsible and accountable is liberating. Once you understand this you will feel how much control you have over your life.*
- *If you are not where you want be, look in the mirror, and that my friend can be the only culprit. If you are reading this, then you are deciding to control your destiny to change your life, for a better more abnormal experience.*

Chapter 35: Describing What We Do

"I build marketing businesses that market for other businesses…or something…right?"
~Justin A. Spencer

How do you explain to someone what it is you do for a living?

More often than I would like, I have found myself struggling to come up with a meaningful description to describe what it is I do to make money.

I remember the first time I was harassed over and over again at a family reunion right after I had dropped out of college and quit my jobs working at Cracker Barrel and Best Buy. Everyone was curious about how I was making money and the best way I could describe it was, "Err, I'm sending web traffic to other companies and they pay me."

Thankfully, the other day I decided to tackle this small obstacle and clear up a few things with my own psyche, so I now know how to better describe what is that I do. I wanted to come up with a definition that accomplished three things.

1) The definition needed to be short.
2) The definition needed to be extremely easy to understand.
3) The definition had to sound cool.

Here is what I came up with (feel free to use this)!

"I have multiple marketing businesses that sell products and services on the internet while I sleep or go on vacation."

I felt that this sentence accomplished the three things I wanted to achieve. I hope this doesn't offend anyone. Honestly sometimes when you tell the truth, people think you are bragging, when in reality you are simply explaining a benefit of your time and energy well spent.

I expect a few of you to think, or say: "badass." It is even more "badass" when you say it say it out loud real quick. Get familiar with it. Next time you find yourself trying to explain to a friend or family member how you are earning so much money, feel free to use that description as an explanatory tool!

Before I continue, I want to answer a question that might be ringing in your head either consciously or sub-consciously. Either way, I would like to address it for you.

If you have multiple marketing businesses, what exactly is a business?

My take on a "business" vs. a "sales site"

I do not consider a "product or service referral website" also know as an "affiliate website" or a "sales site" an ideal business because you do not have control. A sales website may produce revenue from sales your site refers to other businesses, but you do not have control over what you are selling.

Unfortunately, a sales site is more like a virtual salesperson, which means your site is basically employed by the company. When you are employed by anyone, you are not a business. You are simply a minion of the real business; your duty is to make them money while you get paid left over scraps.

"Sales sites" or "Affiliate sites" imply that you do not own the products or services the sites are selling, so they are more like employees or tireless virtual salespeople for the business you are marketing. One could argue that being an affiliate is in fact the business of marketing for businesses. Which is true, but it doesn't possess the main quality of a business which is ownership or control, which you have little of since you are doing the selling and not the product creation.

As an affiliate, you do not determine the product price or the service costs; you do not throw new services and products into the marketplace. You are highly dependent on the company you are marketing for. You rely on them to *not* change the "affiliate terms" that they are in control of; and you rely on them to stay in business so that your income remains intact.

Established brands have canceled their affiliate programs because they simply did not need them. GameVance.com canceled their affiliate program simply because they were growing so rapidly on their own that they did not need affiliates to stimulate their business.

Now imagine if their program was your bread and butter? True entrepreneurship is being the boss and actually being in control over your business and ultimately your life.

I would like to briefly touch upon another topic that is extremely relevant to your focus and success as an online entrepreneur. You may or may not have heard of the phrase "Shiny Object Syndrome".

You have to understand something right away if you are going to be in this business. The online atmosphere is an ever changing, continually expanding and moving target. New innovations, thoughts, and re-branded methodologies of marketing on the internet are released every single day.

Each claims to be the "next new thing" when in reality it is the same exact thing as every other thing with one small ingredient changed. This is normally the name of the product and/or an additional feature or twist or spin.

I have purchased dozens of the latest shiny objects, not because I am interested in them, but simply because I like to know how other marketers are thinking and the trends that marketing products could potentially be opening.

As a beginner, intermediate or expert online business owner, it is important to stay away from diversification. What this means is this: there are multiple ways to advertise on the internet to get customers and make money. Don't try to be an expert at all of them—at least not at the same time.

If you want to succeed you need to select one focus or one business model that you like for whatever which reason and you focus solely on that. Once you master one method of internet advertising then expand your horizon and focus on another until you master it.

This doesn't mean you can't familiarize yourself with different methodologies; obviously you have to in order to decide which type of business model you would like to select. The key is to focus on one model at a time. Jumping back and forth won't do much.

I believe Warren Buffet said something among the lines of, "Do what you know and do it well".

Warren Buffet can rightfully assume if a business is worth buying or not. His multi-billion dollar empire demonstrates that he knows what he is investing in. Warren Buffet does only this and he does it well. Some may think his judgment powers in reference to analyzing a business are a gift from God. Although it is possible that could be a small piece of it, based on what I know about him, I feel that he would care to explain that it is a result of practice, mistakes, accountability and repetition.

Donald Trump is another multi-billionaire. What does the Donald do? He buys real estate and he transforms whatever real estate he buys into something more valued then what it was before. Donald doesn't just buy real estate, however his vast comprehension of developing real estate has been a key component that led to much of his financial success.

When you find someone who is simply "good at everything", please be sure to write me a letter to let me know. You may meet someone who appears to "know everything" but they certainly are not "good at everything". Big difference.

My point is this: master one art before you move on to the next.

Believe me, I have tried to do everything at the same time and I can happily tell you that scattering and diversifying your energy into different places instead of channeling it into one single objective at a time will not be nearly as effective.

Remember: "Do what you know and do it well"

After you master one model, attack the next. Just remember to get tunnel vision and that it is the small, commonly missed details that yield the big results. You will not see the small details in either model if you are not focused.

***

Connecting the dots:

- *Owning an online business means we market (sell) stuff via websites.*
- *Affiliate sites give you limited control because you do not own the product or service you are selling.*
- *Get tunnel vision: familiarize yourself with your options then select one focus.*
- *You will miss the small details that yield big results if you are not focused on one business model or art form.*

Chapter 36: On Connections

"Business is all about who you know."
~Anonymous

The above quote is normally verbalized by individuals who make excuses. The quote implies that you have to be lucky to be successful or to make your fortune. However, I do not disagree with the quote as a whole.

Your success in business is not determined by who you know, but rather, what you believe.

When you make important business connections, it gives you the ability to amplify or scale your business. It does not matter if you are best friends with Bill Gates. That does not automatically mean you are going to be able lead an extremely successful life in business or in general.

Your belief system will dictate how you run your business and the numbers your business produces, whether they are green or red.

On that same note, the ability to create business connections is an asset that is indispensable. Making connections with other likeminded business owners who know how to get things done, like you, will give you new opportunities to potentially put your business on steroids.

I'm going to ask you to do something that will surely brush you outside of your comfort zone. Talk to someone tomorrow that you do not know. Strike up a conversation out of the blue and see what happens. It's even better if you strike up a conversation with someone outside your work background (not a co worker).

The more you do this; the more you will become aware of two things:

1) Doors will open and new opportunities will become available to **you**
2) These opportunities can **positively** impact your life, on a scale you may have never thought possible

Oprah Winfrey said, "I believe luck is preparation meeting opportunity. If you hadn't been prepared when the opportunity came along, you wouldn't have been lucky."

Let me share a quick story with you.

A little less than a year ago I met two individuals who were extremely successful with their business.

Exactly 354 days ago, I met two gifted internet entrepreneurs who generated no less than a quarter million dollars per month of revenue. Their business model is completely relevant to this book, because the methods in which they earn their money are a great example of some of the key aspects I discuss with you, which are: providing a huge amount of value to a vast audience.

What do they do? They are problem solvers, who know how to market solutions to problems, very well, using the internet. They are also teachers, in their own right; they host seminars, and travel across the planet sharing their secrets to success that have made them millions. These two guys could choose to never work again, however they have too much love for the game to quit.

In any case, I met with these two individuals on a private basis because I wanted to breathe the same air they were breathing, I wanted to see them in person, I wanted to see the two individuals who were not shackled to the financial barriers most people are restricted to.

At what cost? Money was a factor, but for the small price I paid, the over-arching outcome was nothing short of life changing.

I attended the meeting with my primary objective being: to notice everything that these guys did. How they spoke, how they thought, how they attacked problems, what their opinions were and how they viewed things. You name it; every word was carefully documented in my brain or on paper.

Little did I know, my enthusiasm and my similar passion for the game of business was planting a transparent seed that would ultimately fast forward my roadmap to success in business by at least one year.

At the end of our private meeting, one of the two guys revealed to me that he lived in New York; obviously these guys keep a low profile on where they live, and for good reason. I currently live in New York.

He liked my enthusiasm, he saw a spark and he offered me a job to work for him, in the same exact office. This is a perfect example of preparation meeting opportunity. Although my car didn't start after the meeting ended, I realized my life was about to change, for keeps.

Now I know what you may be thinking: "Justin is successful because he got hired to work for a millionaire."

For those of you who entertained this thought, allow me to clarify something: I do not make well into the 5 figure per month mark because of that event.

I had established an outgoing, and enthusiastic attitude beforehand and I prepared myself for the opportunity, so in essence I created my own luck.

One of the gentlemen actually told me later on, "You would have been successful with or without us bro." (Obviously these guys are very personable)

What this opportunity did do for me was this: It significantly reduced the amount of time it would take me to achieve things.

No one gave me a golden map and compass to find success and this is largely due to the fact that these two items do not exist. I now had a new employer, as well as a friend to help guide my compass, but I still had to draw the map. He recommended books for me to read, and he would give me little details in regards to how to execute tasks. In essence, he gave me all of the tools I needed to build my gun.

But he left it to me to pull the trigger.

He knew I had what it took; he knew that I was a walker, not just a dreamer.

***

Connecting the dots:

- *Business is not about who you know. Business is about what you believe.*
- *When preparation meets opportunity, you become lucky.*
- *Having business connections is an indispensable asset.*
- *Breathing the same air as other successful business owners will have a positive impact on you.*
- *Connecting with successful, likeminded people who share your passions can create an infinite world of possibilities.*
- *Making a great impression and demonstrating enthusiasm will create more opportunities and it's always in your favor to be passionate!*

Chapter 37: On Sales Process

"Quality is never an accident; it is always the result of high intention, sincere effort, intelligent direction and skillful execution; it represents the wise choice of many alternatives."
~ Willa A. Foster

Creating a high quality, intelligent sales process requires time and skillful execution. It requires careful thought and it makes your business an 800 pound gorilla of a competitor instead of a 100 pound monkey.

Many individuals hear the term sales process, and the true meaning of what sales process stands for does not ring in their heads to the tune that it should.

Your sales process is perhaps the most vital part of your internet business. Without a competent sales process in place, your chances of experiencing success with what you are trying to sell will be simplified to a small percent.

Are you willing to face those types of odds? Succeeding in business is all about taking whatever it is you have and using it to your advantage, sprinkling in a few creative ideas and seasoning your process with some innovative execution to materialize your successful business.

A sales process is your diagram, or mind map of the objectives you are going to achieve, with real plays or processes involved to make those objectives become real.

What should your objective be?

In business, your objective should be this, or something around or near this: To provide more value to your customers than your competitors, to establish a presence in the marketplace that sheds positive opinions about your company or brand and to squeeze as much money as possible out of your customers by making offers to them that only an idiot would refuse.

How do we make these objectives become a reality? By creating and testing and refining a solid sales process. If your sales process is considered the heart of your business, then your business model would have to be considered the brains.

The business model determines how a sales process will take form.

Your business model will be based on the type of product or service you offer. If the service that you offer is a subscription-based service, then you receive a monthly reoccurring payment from each of your subscribers (customers).

Netflix is a good example. They charge $8 per month if I am not mistaken, for providing tremendous value to their customers. Although Netflix has made mistakes in the past by not placing the customers as their main stakeholder, if I remember correctly, they readjusted the price of their service back to the way it was before they split into two entities.

Stakeholders are the building blocks that drive business. A stakeholder can be your customer, a venture capitalist, or a stock investor—it's someone who contributes to the success of the business.

Netflix made the mistake of responding to demands made by investors who bought shares within the company, and as a result they changed their business model to satisfy the investors, to stimulate the returns the investors desired. Not only did this backfire on returns for the investors, but many loyal Netflix customers were outraged and discontinued their service with Netflix. You need to know that your most important stakeholder is your customer, always. You customers come first because they drive your business—end of story.

So if your business model is to offer a service that requires monthly recurring payments such as Netflix, then you can dictate how to establish your sales process with this knowledge.

For example, if Netflix on average can determine, based on their customer data, that each person who signs up with Netflix keeps the service for two years, then they can draw some powerful information that can be integrated into their sales process.

If on average, a Netflix customer stays with the service for two years, that means that 8 * 24 = $192, and that is what an average customer is worth. Since Netflix charges $8/mo, what does this mean in terms of how it affects their sales process?

Simple – they can afford to spend more money getting new customers because they know that if it costs them $150 in advertising spending to gain one customer, then they are creating a profit or more cash inflow then outflow. Even if they are losing $150 upfront, they will not only recover that investment back, but they will profit it from it in the future as well.

So a business with this type of model can change their sales process to involve spending a heavy amount of money to obtain new customers.

This is why your competitors on Google Adwords can spend $20 a click. Your competitors have business models that allow them to develop a sales process where they can still profit while outbidding you by $18 and stealing all of the customers in the process, no pun intended.

One common mistake marketers and entrepreneurs make is spending more time and energy getting a new customer instead of nurturing the relationship with your existing customer. Gaining a new loyal customer as opposed to marketing to an already existing loyal customer is more difficult.

This is why sales processes can be changed, critiqued and improved over time. Maybe your sales process in the beginning will be to gain as many loyal customers to start, then later on when you have a loyal customer base, your sales process focus will be to provide more value to existing customers. Give your existing customers rewards, perks and bonuses for being a loyal customer.

Know when to critique or improve the focus of your sales process. More money and value can be made by marketing to existing customers than to take out your wallet and spend $150 for a new customer worth $192.

You can offer your existing customer base more services and increase the value of each loyal customer you already have instead of spending a fortune to get new customers.

Profiting $42 over 2 years, or profiting $240,000 in 30 days? It's all about leveraging what you already have. Adjust your sales process. It is like fashion—it never will be perfect nor will it ever end. There is always an adjustment that can be made to your sales process, whether it is better customer service to keep your average loyal customer longer, or whether it is critiquing your service or products to provide more value so you can charge more.

Keep your mind churning on these three things:

1) Identifying potential weaknesses in your sales process
2) Brainstorming possible solutions that eliminate weaknesses and add value
3) Brilliantly executing and integrating the solution into your process

The result? A better, more improved sales process that generates more revenue, more profit and more value to your customers, it's a win/win situation.

What if your business model is not based on selling a monthly subscriber based service? First, you should consider adding a service to your business to incorporate a monthly re-bill product/service to create more cash inflow. Why? Is it worth your time to provide something of value to a loyal customer base that will pay you and fill your fridge with food each month?

Yeah, it is. Hell yeah, it is.

If your business model involves selling pots and pans, then you are likely targeting people who either like to cook or have to cook because that is their role in the household. Therefore they need a good product to allow them to do so.

Or likewise, you can do B2B (business to business) selling, and you can sell to restaurant owners.

For the sake of this example let's say your ideal audience or prospects are restaurant owners who see the value in investing in exceptional cookware.

In your sales process, the first step should be not necessarily to pitch your product. The first step in this type of business model should be to earn your customers' trust in order to sell them something of overwhelming value later.

Why not offer your website visitors who are either potentially cooking enthusiasts, or restaurant owners / managers a free professionally drafted cookbook by the top chefs in the world? How in the world do you obtain an exclusive book drafted by the best cooks in the world? Once again a brilliant idea needs brilliant execution and for that I leave you decide.

However, realistically speaking I can assure you that you that you can provide something much easier to create that amounts to the same perceived value. The idea is to provide something exceptional to cut through the noise. You can write your own cookbook if you are knowledgeable on the subject or you can hire someone to do so.

Revaluing this free offer to your prospect requires use of particular words that will compel your prospect to trade his/her personal information for your free cookbook.

Use sales copy similar to this:

Targeting restaurant owners: "Learn 3 Cooking Secrets that Will Make Your Customers Mouths Water and Compel Them to Keep Coming Back for Your Exclusive Recipes"

Targeting cooking enthusiasts or individuals who cook out of desire or necessity: "Learn 3 Cooking Secrets that Will Make Your Spouse and Kids Obey Your Every Command in Exchange for Your Taste Bud Shocking Meals"

In exchange for this compelling offer you can gain the persons following information:

- Enter: First name
- Enter: Email Address
- Enter: Phone Number (Optional)
- Enter: Address (Optional)
- Enter: Zip and State (Optional)

Even though you label half of the fields optional and the only requirements are name and email, you will find a percentage of people willing to give you all of their information.

The more information they provide, the more valuable the customer is because you can market to this customer through email and by direct mail as well as by phone if you so decide. Once you have the person's information you can always sell them anything related to cooking and beyond.

This type of business model dictates how the sales process is created which is to:

1) Offer a compelling free product in exchange for your prospects' info.
2) Email a follow up with the person and deliver on your promise.
3) Send meaningful emails and/or direct mail to provide value or free offers to your customers. This will build trust and a strong, positive relationship.
4) Market to your emailing list, send direct mail to promote your products, and make compelling offers by advertising the reduced price your loyal customers are required to pay as opposed to the public price for "non-loyal" customers.

5) You have these people for as long as you are willing to keep them. By adding value to their day, you can create income in your pocket.

So the moral here is, whether you are selling particular products or a recurring service or whether you are brokering services by connecting buyers to sellers, your sales process will always be based on your business model.

Know that your sales process can always be improved, critiqued and refined to provide more value to your existing customers and to obtain new loyal customers at a lower expense.

Creating a brilliant sales process does take time, but if took you 3 years to create a successful sales process for your business model that yields a $250,000 profit per year, is that worth it?

Would you rather spend 40 years working for someone else to save up $500,000 towards your retirement so you can enjoy 10 years before you leave this planet? I'm not going to apologize for being brash. 3 years is a small tradeoff for financial freedom.

A "back end" is a piece of your sales process where you make money by providing substantial value to your existing customers. Likewise the "front end" is your cost per new customer or cost per first sale. When people think of business, they collectively think "my cash inflow has to be greater than my cash outflow" or that the revenue must be greater than the expenses.

As with the Netflix example, you can afford to spend $150 to earn $8 back each month from one customer. When your business model has a sales process that allows this structure, you create a profit.

After you determine your business model, you can create blueprints for your sales process. Remember, when you are thinking about how to frame your sales process, you have to keep the following things in mind:

1) What steps can I take to make sure I provide the most value possible to my customers?
2) What weaknesses do my competitors have they I can capitalize on? Or in other words, what are my competitors doing wrong that I can do right, or what are my competitors doing now that I can do better, or improve upon?
3) How should I market my products to my customers in a way that aligns with my revenue goals while still providing value unequaled by my competitors or anyone remotely close to my industry?

If these compelling questions are addressed and brilliantly executed into your business model's sales process, I promise that you will get results.

This also means that you will not create a perfect sales process your first time around, or your second time around. But you can create a decent sales process the third time around that does produce numbers.

Then you can critique, refine and improve your process to make it even better and better.

Take away points from this chapter:

1) Decide what your business model is. You can do this by determining what it is you're selling: whether it is a product or service or both. Remember to study your market prior to entry. Know what your competitors are doing and understand what they are doing well and what they are doing badly.

2) Define your objectives with your service or product. These objectives will serve as your roots for the creation of your sales process. Develop your unique sales proposition (USP) which separates your business or brand from your competitors. Offer something of incredible value and capitalize on what your competitors do a bad job with.

3) Once you execute your sales process based on your business model and company goals and objectives, look at the numbers, identify strong and weak points and improve upon your process, continually and religiously.

Your competitors, if they are smart, will also be adapting their sales process. You will find that they will copy you when they notice your process works better. Fear not, because you are the innovator, and you are a step ahead. They are following you and trailing behind you.

Likewise, study your competitors' process and if their process proves to be more sufficient, adjust your model accordingly. There is no such thing as originality in marketing and business. Swipe and deploy.

Focus on improving your process. Sometimes it is necessary to scrap a process, but more often than not it is necessary to isolate the weaknesses of a process and solve those problems to make the process stronger.

***

Connecting the dots:

- *Your business model will determine how you can structure your sales process.*
- *Creating an exceptional sales process is an ongoing task of constant adaptation.*
- *Your process can be framed on the basis of your competitors' faults.*
- *Know your strengths and capitalize on them; isolate your weaknesses and resolve them.*
- *Don't make the classic Netflix mistake—your customers come first.*

"ATTENTION ALL TRAVELERS AND AIRPORT PERSONEL, ALL SCHEDULED FLIGHTS ARE NOW PREPARING TO BOARD."

"Well then, I guess that is our cue." Justin said.

He smiled and looked at me right in the eye and said, "I believe in you."

"I know you can take what I have taught you today and do well for yourself and others.

Remember, focus, discipline and passion.

Those three things will help you manifest anything you desire in life, *not* just successfully creating marketing businesses on the internet.

So long, my friend, it was nice meeting you.

I hope we will meet again someday and I cannot wait to hear what you have become—make me proud."

After he said this, I thanked him and he walked towards his plane to take off.

And just like that, he was gone…on his way to his next adventure.

I could not believe what Justin had just told me.

I walked towards the docking station where my flight was soon to depart.

The darkened skyline started to become illuminated with light. I watched as the sky became full of light and energy. I stared out the transparent glass of the airport that separated me from the world. I watched as a plane cruised up the airstrip preparing to take off and emerge into the sky and I thought about him.

I thought about what Justin went through and I thought about what he had become.

The **light** from the glass reflected towards me, and a smile crossed my face.

I could not get rid of that smile if I had tried.

I felt invincible.

I realized I had a choice.

Now. It is **my** turn.

"Get the Right Information, the Right Examples and the Right Action Steps, to Start Making Money Online Immediately"

www.ForeverProfitSystem.com

What do *you* get?

1. Over *15 hours* of lecture style and computer *screen captured footage* showing how to implement every process in this book.
2. *Exclusive* website templates that I use to make over *$1,000 profit per day* ***(Free)***
3. *Insider trade secrets* about internet marketing (worth the price of the course alone)
4. A *permanent* discount on the Gold membership club (more down below)
5. An exclusive *chance* to receive a *1 on 1* workshop with Justin.
6. An enhanced outlook and *invaluable skill set* for making money not just on the internet, but in all different professions and walks of life.
7. ***Financial Freedom by mixing education with action.***

Take action today:

www.ForeverProfitSystem.com

It is Your turn.

Be Great.

Stay *Connected* with Justin and *Learn* More:

www.ForeverProfitSystem.com

www.iJustinSpencer.com

www.Twitter.com/spencify

Printed in Dunstable, United Kingdom

91222513R00136